THE
Philanthropist
Handbook

FINDING MEANING IN THE
ENDOWMENT OF HUMANITY

THE
Philanthropist
Handbook

CLAY M. GRAYSON

Advantage | Books

Published by Advantage Books, Charleston, South Carolina.
An imprint of Advantage Media.

ADVANTAGE is a registered trademark, and the Advantage colophon is a trademark of Advantage Media Group, Inc.

Printed in the United States of America.

10 9 8 7 6 5 4 3 2 1

ISBN: 979-8-89188-073-3 (Paperback)
ISBN: 979-8-89188-074-0 (Hardcover)
ISBN: 979-8-89188-075-7 (eBook)

Library of Congress Control Number: 2024916987

Cover design by Analisa Smith.
Layout design by Ruthie Wood.

This publication is designed to provide accurate and authoritative information in regard to the subject matter covered. It is sold with the understanding that the publisher is not engaged in rendering legal, accounting, or other professional services. If legal advice or other expert assistance is required, the services of a competent professional person should be sought.

Advantage Books is an imprint of Advantage Media Group. Advantage Media helps busy entrepreneurs, CEOs, and leaders write and publish a book to grow their business and become the authority in their field. Advantage authors comprise an exclusive community of industry professionals, idea-makers, and thought leaders. For more information go to **advantagemedia.com**.

This book is dedicated to my mentor and friend,

F. Mitchell Johnson, Jr.

CONTENTS

ACKNOWLEDGMENTS. IX

PREFACE XI

PART 1 1
The Philanthropic Role in Society

CHAPTER 1 3
Are You a Philanthropist?
Our Charitable Nature 4
What's in a Word? 5

CHAPTER 2 11
The Nonprofit in American Society
Churches and Religious Organizations. 13
Schools and Educational Organizations. 14
Hospitals and Healthcare Providers 16
How We Got Here. 16
The Modern American Nonprofit 20
Trendlines 21

CHAPTER 3 . . . . **27**

Why Do Nonprofits Exist within Capitalism?

The Relationship of the Philanthropist and the Nonprofit . . .28

Philanthropy as a Basis for Ethics in Capitalist Society 30

Our Nonprofit Champions 36

PART 2 . . . . **39**

Living Philanthropically

CHAPTER 4 . . . .**41**

Philanthropy as a Form of Self-Improvement

Exercises to Align Yourself in the Philanthropic Way 45

CHAPTER 5 . . . . **47**

The Discipline of Empathy

Practice Gratitude. 48

Practice Generosity 50

Read 52

Travel. 53

Practice Listening 54

Make Everything You Do Important. 55

Establish Boundaries 55

How Does the Power of Empathy Support You in Your

Philanthropic Way?. 56

CHAPTER 6 . . . . **59**

The Ethics of Information and Truth

Biases in the Structuring of Data into Information 63

Beware the Power of Philanthropy 66

CHAPTER 7 . . . . **69**
The Discipline of Foresight

CHAPTER 8 . . . . **75**
How Does the Way of Philanthropy Assist
You in Your Role as Philanthropist?

PART 3 . . . . **79**
The Aspirational Nonprofit

CHAPTER 9 . . . .**81**
Designing the Contemporary Nonprofit Organization

CHAPTER 10 . . . . **89**
Evaluating Nonprofit Organizations
  Organizational Learning and Institutional Knowledge *90*
  What Is the Standard to Measure a Nonprofit? *91*

CHAPTER 11 . . . . **95**
Assessing Organizational Learning—Nonprofit Leadership
  What Are the Leadership Roles of a Nonprofit? *95*
  Succession Planning. *98*
  Governance Committee. *99*
  Term Limits *100*
  Annual Director and Officer Pledge. *101*
  Leadership Reflection. *102*

CHAPTER 12. . . . . **105**
Assessing Institutional Knowledge—Internal Controls
  The True Achievement of Accountability *107*

CHAPTER 13 111

Objective Measures of Nonprofits

Reading the Form 990 Tax Return and Audited Financial Statements 112

The Value of Metrics 120

CHAPTER 14 123

Why Are Philanthropists Attracted to Endowments?

Establishing Endowments 125

Internal Controls around Endowments 127

Alignment of Endowment Investment and Charitable Mission 129

Program-Related and Mission-Related Investments 132

The Democratization of the Endowment 136

PART 4 139

Your Philanthropic Plan

CHAPTER 15 141

The Beaufort Fund

The Moseses' Philanthropic Plan 150

Secret Millionaires Next Door 151

Award Committee 152

Trust Philanthropy 153

CHAPTER 16 157

Envisioning Your Philanthropic Plan

Identifying the Nonprofits That Share Your Mission 159

CHAPTER 17 163

Your Philanthropic Team

The Development Officer. 164

The Attorney. 166

The Financial Planner. 167

The Certified Public Accountant. 168

Your Family. 170

Team Insights 171

CHAPTER 18 173

Assets to Fund Your Philanthropic Plan

Categories of Assets 174

CHAPTER 19 179

The Format and Drafting of Your Plan

Gift Agreement 180

Will. 180

Trust Agreement 181

Charitable Remainder Trusts 181

Charitable Lead Trust. 182

Charitable Gift Annuity. 183

Life Insurance 184

Life Insurance Policy Designation 184

Retirement Accounts 184

Bargain Sale 185

Other Legal Documents. 186

CHAPTER 20 189

Endowment Giving within Your Philanthropic Plan

Modification Provisions in Gift Agreements and

Endowments 190

CHAPTER 21 . . . . **195**

Your Message to the Future

Naming Rights *197*

Remembering Those We Love *198*

CHAPTER 22 . . . . **201**

Why We Are Philanthropists

The Philanthropic Way *203*

AFTERWORD **207**

ACKNOWLEDGMENTS

I'd like to first acknowledge and thank my sons, Alex and Rivers, who took such an interest in the book that delighted and, on the hard days, inspired me to finish. I started writing this book when you were five and now, at the time of publication, you are ten. In that time, I watched you learn to read and become aware of and, hopefully, in love with books. I'd like to think that your memories of our discussing the need for an afterword or how the cover art might look will inspire you years from now in your own creative endeavors. I also hope that it may inspire you on your own discovery of philanthropy.

I'd like to acknowledge and thank my wife, Manoli, who inspires me in everything I do. I hope you will consider adding *The Philanthropist Handbook* to one of your many book clubs.

I want to acknowledge my mom, Hope, who first taught me of philanthropy, and my father, Michael, who taught me the discipline to make excellence a habit.

I'd like to thank Bill Moses and Anne McCaffrey for speaking to me about their parents, Alan and Joanne Moses, and graciously permitting me to tell their story. I'd like to thank the Coastal Community Foundation of South Carolina who permitted me to write of CCF's collaboration with the Moses to create the Beaufort Fund, a field of interest fund at CCF to support nonprofits in the counties of Beaufort, Jasper, Hampton, and Colleton, South Carolina.

I could not write a book about philanthropy without acknowledging and thanking Madeleine McGee. Madeleine, I have learned so much about philanthropy, service, and nonprofit organizations from you. Your care, dedication, and thoughtfulness have nurtured a landscape of healthy nonprofit organizations across the state of South Carolina, whose impact will be felt into the next century.

I want to thank all of my clients, the nonprofit leaders, and the many boards with whom I work. You are the inspiration behind many of the ideas in this book.

Finally, I'd like to acknowledge and thank my colleagues at Grayson Law Firm, who share this journey with me to elevate the entire nonprofit sector with the tools, skills, and thought leadership that each nonprofit may achieve mission success.

PREFACE

As the baby boomers reach their golden years, we're beginning to experience the greatest transition of generational wealth we've ever seen in the United States. Over the next twenty years, it's anticipated that this generation may pass down as much as $12 trillion in charitable contributions to nonprofits. Perhaps more meaningfully, of that $12 trillion, up to $9.6 trillion, or 80 percent of all these charitable contributions, could be done through planned gifts. And of these planned gifts, most donors want their contributions going into endowments, where the corpus of the gift will be restricted forever but the annual income arising therefrom will be distributed for charitable purposes.[1]

A few things strike me here. First, the size of this generational transfer to charity is incredible: "To understand the scale of this change, consider that in 2020 all U.S. foundations together distributed about $472 billion in grants. Adjust for these figures for inflation,

---

1   Ben Eisen and Anne Tergesen, "Older Americans Stockpiled a Record $35 Trillion. The Time Has Come to Give It Away," *The Wall Street Journal*, July 2, 2021, https://www.wsj.com/articles/older-americans-35-trillion-wealth-giving-away-heirs-philanthropy-11625234216.

and you are still looking at enough fuel to drive philanthropy for more than a century."[2]

The other thing to consider is that planned gifts are gifts made at death. Eighty percent of this generational wealth transfer is predicted to be made in wills, trusts, or something similar.

A certain psychology of reckoning is going on here. For most of us, as we age, we start to think about what follows after. Many of us have profound religious beliefs about what comes next. Others are looking to right wrongs during life before we go. Many are thinking about their legacy and what kind of lasting impact they will have on the world after they're gone. You can look at a planned gift as a measure of good that you put into this world. It's a chance to balance the scales, make penance, or make a real difference.

All of us know we can't take it with us. When your survival is no longer important, how do you view wealth? Your answer says a lot about you.

While it's a big deal when an individual gives away a double-digit percentage of their wealth to charity, what does it say about the person who wants the corpus of the gift to remain invested forever, with only the annual income to be distributed for a charitable purpose? It intrigues me that so many baby boomers might be drawn to make planned gifts to endowments. This is an investment in humanity's future. It's as if, from a lifetime of work, this is your contribution for all who follow. The widespread attraction to endowments says something about our nature.

---

2   "A Look at Generational Changes in Philanthropy and Giving Practices," Giving Compass, November 8, 2023, https://givingcompass.org/article/a-look-at-generational-changes-in-philanthropy-and-giving-practices#:~:text=For%20 example%2C%20older%20individuals%20are,through%20these%20traditional%20 contribution%20avenues.

I became interested in this subject by way of a drift into which my career fell. I am a tax attorney who went to NYU law school and then returned to my hometown of Charleston, South Carolina, to practice law in the early 2000s. I took a job as an associate with a notable public finance and bond law firm. In connection with our work, I was taught to vet nonprofit organizations. I had to write opinions about the ability and authority of these organizations to enter into various types of transactions. In turn, lenders or investors relied on our review of these organizations and our written opinions regarding their strengths and weaknesses. This work enabled universities to build new dormitories and academic medical centers to build hospitals and surgical centers. In those early days, I also began to work with nonprofit research foundations of universities as they attempted to license technology outward to the market. Over time, the endowment foundations found me, and I started helping them draft investment policy statements and consider mitigation strategies to reduce or eliminate unrelated business income tax arising from their investments.

I did that work for a long time. But things started to change. The clients whom I was helping to build dormitories on university campuses or surgical centers for academic medical centers started reaching out to me with more and more questions. I started drifting away from transactional and finance-related work. I became more involved in client operations. In time, my role evolved to become an external general counsel for hire for nonprofits.

And I started going to board meetings … a lot of board meetings. I attend at least 125 board meetings per year. Considering there are fifty-two weeks in each year, it's not as bad as it seems. Videoconferencing helps.

The relationships I began to develop with directors on these boards also changed. They became some of the more meaningful relationships in my adult life. Many of these individuals were retired, and nonprofit service was a second career. As I worked with them and got to know them better, I started seeing many of these individuals as my mentors and a few as true friends.

If you keep hearing discussions, time after time, at board meetings about mission, vision, and values, and if these are authentic discussions, you start learning a lot about integrity and living for a purpose greater than yourself. As I listened to people I respected and cared for talk about mission, I couldn't help but think about my own mission. *What am I doing in this world?* As I got older, that question started to affect me.

In 2018, I opened a start-up law firm, with the goal of providing services only to nonprofits and philanthropists. Every aspect of my firm was to go toward service as a nonprofit general counsel for hire. I had drifted into my swim lane, and it felt like a new lease on life.

Today, my firm represents over four hundred nonprofits across much of the United States. A lot of my job nowadays is teaching younger attorneys how to represent nonprofits. But what I still get to do, and what I love to do, is to work side by side with development officers, helping philanthropists make significant gifts to nonprofits. In this role, I've found conversations with individuals considering a planned gift to one of my clients to be among the most personal and real. These are the conversations that stay with me. We don't live life with a singular goal to make a planned gift. It's mostly when we near the end that we begin to think about this type of thing. A certain honesty in our self-reflection emerges when we begin to think about life and death in terms of a planned gift.

I also see other commonalities in these conversations. Over life, most of us have a history of charitable giving with the nonprofits to which we will leave a planned gift. Many of the people with whom I speak have personal relationships with the development officers, the boards, and the leaders of these nonprofits. At one point or another, many have served as a director or officer in those organizations. In all instances, their lives have been touched, and they desire to give back.

A planned gift makes a nonprofit your heir, a part of your family. Nonprofit relationships are family relationships.

Planned gifts don't come out of nowhere. They're the manifestation of a lifetime of an individual's philanthropy. I think that's why I'm captivated by this historic generational transfer of wealth to nonprofits. It seems to prove that philanthropy exists in each of us.

As I look at my friends, I see many of the activities occurring at younger stages of life that will later inspire a planned gift. I see donations. I see board service. I see individuals standing up to volunteer. All around, I see younger versions of those same baby boomers who now are talking with me about planned giving. I see the possibility to tap into the philanthropy that exists in each of us from the day we were born.

Ultimately, all of us have the capacity to be philanthropists. A philanthropist is *an empathetic individual who not only performs charitable actions but does so with foresight oriented toward a plan to maximize impact*. A successful philanthropic plan will continue to fulfill its mission long after the philanthropist has passed away. Indeed, a fair way to evaluate an individual's success is whether, from a lifetime of philanthropic investment, the return arising after death exceeds the volume of the world's resources such individual consumed during life.

Drawing from my years working as an attorney for nonprofits and the lessons I've learned from so many directors, leaders, and consultants, I wrote this handbook to inspire you to be a philanthropist. It doesn't matter your age, your background, or your bank account. This handbook is designed to provide something for everyone. I hope it will inspire you to find your personal vision of philanthropy. I hope it will also give you the tools and the acumen to maximize the impact of your vision for generations to come.

In terms of its outline, this handbook is organized into four parts.

Part 1 examines the role of philanthropy in democratic capitalist societies from a historical perspective, with an emphasis on its socioeconomic effects. We will examine the charitable nature inherent to humans and look for a definition of the word *philanthropy*. And we will ask the following question: Why do nonprofits exist in capitalist societies?

Part 2 is an introduction to the philanthropic way. It is designed to help you identify and cultivate within yourself three disciplines that are of significance to the overall character of a philanthropist: empathy, the ethics of information and truth, and foresight.

In Part 3, we turn our attention to modern nonprofit organizations. This handbook will provide tools and metrics to assess an organization's ability to create an unending return from your philanthropic investment. We will examine a nonprofit organization's potential based on its ability to engage in organizational learning and retain institutional knowledge. We will define success from a long-range perspective, calculating increases or decreases in the intergenerational equity of a nonprofit organization as a means to evaluate performance and impact over time.

Part 4 returns us to your own individual call to philanthropy. It pulls together parts 1 through 3 in order to pursue the creation and memorialization of your own philanthropic plan.

There are times in life when you can reflect on the world around you, how to heal scars and wounds in society, or how you can make a difference in your own way based on your own foresight and personal ethics. In this way, each of us may create our own meaning in life.

Whether you're contemplating service on a board of directors, a career in nonprofit administration, or a significant gift to charity, the purpose of this handbook is to provide you a philanthropist mindset drawn from classical times but that remains important, current, and topical even today.

As you read this handbook, I want you to ask yourself this: "How can I share in the philanthropic experience?" And if more of us ask that question and strive to walk from time to time in the philanthropic way, I think we'll find our world to be a better place. Our conversations may become more civil and our perspective on society more inclusive.

Let this handbook serve as a guide to help you along your own way of philanthropy.

PART 1

The Philanthropic Role in Society

Philanthropy is commendable, but it must not cause the philanthropist to overlook the circumstances of economic injustice that make philanthropy necessary.

—MARTIN LUTHER KING JR.

CHAPTER 1

Are You a Philanthropist?

P*hilanthropist.* The term conjures up many associations: a description at a banquet to honor a noteworthy person, a word used in obituaries. No one takes offense to being called by that name, although some may dismiss it with humility.

I'll tell you a secret. Most everyone is charitable. While human nature may be cruel and evil at times, it also has an inherent ability to care for and protect the weakest of us—the sick, the poor, the elderly, and our children—to have empathy, and to put the needs of others before our own. Make no mistake, being charitable is not the same thing as being a philanthropist. As suggested in the preface, philanthropy requires coupling our charitable nature with foresight and orienting it toward some larger goal. Philanthropy in this fuller sense is an inherent capacity that is available to all of us. A primary goal of this handbook is to help you harness the philanthropy that lies within you in order to amplify its effect with greater meaning and purpose in your life and in the lives of others.

Our Charitable Nature

Most people know Adam Smith as an economist and author of the foundational treatise of modern global capitalism, *The Wealth of Nations*. Fewer people realize that he was also a philosopher of human nature. This was even the foundation of his economics: our nature makes us behave in manner X, and thus we have outcome Y. Smith understood that within capitalism, where supply and labor shift to areas with core competencies in terms of cost, speed, reliability, and quality, the drive for efficiency reigns supreme. Capitalism in its rawest form seeks profit at the cost of all else, including people—especially people. Smith recognized this, but he still believed that capitalism would succeed because he saw other balancing qualities in our nature. He saw empathy in us.

In his *Theory of Moral Sentiments*, Smith wrote of the quality of human beings to feel and empathize with others immediately around us. If you are around someone who is happy, you become happy too. If you are around someone sad, it makes you sad. Our natural core reaction is to comfort the sad person and, if possible, to help them. Adam Smith saw this sympathetic quality to our nature as the key to making capitalism work. He called this our "fellow-feeling." Our charitable nature is the balance in capitalism that binds us together in communities. Without it, competition in its purest sense would tear us apart.

According to Smith, empathy enables us to understand the perspective of others and to share their emotions, which is essential for building strong social bonds and for making ethical decisions. Smith believed that empathy helps us to recognize the needs and interests of others and to act in ways that promote their welfare. He believed this is the basis of moral behavior.

You might view philanthropy as the conscious effort of an individual to harness their charitable nature, this "fellow-feeling," and, more significantly, to direct it through a planned and meaningful engagement with a societal purpose. A philanthropist plans the charitable effort, selecting a cause that reflects the authentic self, and in doing so relinquishes the self in favor of community.

Philanthropy must be more than adding a dollar to your purchase at the grocery store or dropping your spare change in a bucket with some charity as the beneficiary. Being philanthropic is something different. It's a capacity in our nature that we have to cultivate. An individual who is being charitable, while noble and worthy, will lack the direction of a philanthropist and thus will never achieve the impact a philanthropist can achieve through a thoughtful plan, singularly guided with purpose that is grounded in a personal vision and ethos.

For those of you who wish to read on, you have already answered the first question—Are you a philanthropist?—in the affirmative.

What's in a Word?

The word *philanthropy* originates from the ancient Greeks' story of the creation of humankind. It entered our vocabulary twenty-five hundred years ago with its first appearance in the ancient Greek tragedy *Prometheus Bound*, written by the playwright Aeschylus.

In ancient Greek mythology, it was believed that when the gods battled the ancient Titans for dominance of the world, the Titan Prometheus fought on the side of the gods and convinced his brother, Epimetheus, to do the same. The gods overthrew the Titans. Many Titans were killed. The few remaining were imprisoned in a stormy pit known as Tartarus that lay beneath the foundation of Earth.

For their loyalty and as thanks, Zeus tasked Prometheus and his brother with the responsibility to create all living creatures on Earth. They were given a great bag filled with talents from the gods to distribute to their creations. Epimetheus began to create all manner of living things, bestowing on them gifts from the various talents. To some he gave flight, to others the ability to swim beneath water, and to others great strength or speed. Prometheus, on the other hand, focused exclusively on one creature, humans, molding us from clay and water. He formed us in the image of the gods.

When it came time for Prometheus to bestow a gift from the gods upon humanity, he realized that his brother had given out all the talents in their possession. Early humans found themselves disadvantaged in this new world. At night, they hid in caves. During the day, they struggled to compete for food and resources.

To make matters worse, upon reviewing Prometheus's creation, Zeus decreed that humans were to remain mortal and worship the gods in Mount Olympus. They were to be subservient creatures, vulnerable to the elements, and dependent on the gods' mercy for survival.

Distraught, Prometheus sought the counsel of Athena, the goddess of wisdom, as to how he might advantage his creation in this world. Athena advised Prometheus to visit the blacksmith god, Hephaestus, at his workshop and ask him for fire from his forge as a gift to humanity. With fire, humans would be able to advance. They would have light and warmth at night. Prometheus did as Athena advised. The result was as Athena predicted. Humans were able to cook food, create tools, and build shelter, and they began to live together in communities.

Eventually, after watching humans begin to prosper, Zeus asked Prometheus to develop ceremonial forms of animal sacrifice for humans to make in honor of the gods. To advantage humans,

Prometheus devised a trick. He slaughtered a large bull and divided its parts into two presentations for Zeus. The first presentation was the delicious meat of the animal, but the meat was wrapped in the disgusting stomach lining. The second presentation consisted of the bones wrapped in a thick layer of rich fat. One offering was to be made for the gods, and the other offering was to be kept by humanity for making the sacrifice. Prometheus presented to Zeus the following decision: Which of the two would go to the gods and which to man? Zeus took the rich-appearing presentation—the fat-encased but inedible bones. Prometheus tricked Zeus out of the best portion of the sacrificial feast, granting meat for the benefit of humankind.

In anger, as punishment Zeus removed fire from humanity. He forbade humans from using fire to cook meat or for any other purpose. Quickly, humans regressed to their prior meager existence.

Prometheus found this outcome unacceptable. He refused to see his creation denied this resource. One night, he scaled Mount Olympus and sneaked into Hephaestus's workshop. There, he stole fire from the forge, concealed it in a hollow stalk of fennel, and returned it to humanity. With fire, humans were able to resume their rapid progression toward civilization and eventual dominance of the natural world.

His pride hurt for the last time, Zeus ordered Hephaestus to take Prometheus into custody, carry him to Mount Caukasos, and nail him to a pillar thereupon. Every day thereafter, Zeus would set a vulture to feed upon Prometheus's liver. Being a Titan, Prometheus's liver would regenerate each day, only to be set upon, causing agonizing pain, again and again.

It's rumored that Zeus would come to Prometheus from time to time and offer to release the Titan if Prometheus would agree to take fire from humanity. The story goes that Prometheus refused, accepting his sacrifice for his children.

The term *philanthropy* originated to describe Prometheus's feelings and relationship to us, his creation, his children. Prometheus loved us. He defied Zeus, and he suffered for us. In *Prometheus Bound*, primitive humans had no knowledge, skills, or culture. We were living in dark caves. Aeschylus wrote that Prometheus, out of his *philanthropos tropos* ("humanity-loving character"), gave fire to humanity, symbolizing all knowledge, skills, technology, arts, and science. Prometheus endowed humanity with "blind hope" through optimism. With optimism, we use fire to improve the human condition. With fire, we may see the light in the darkness.

Aeschylus's new word, *philanthropos*, was a portmanteau, a combination of the word *philos*, meaning loving in the sense of benefiting, caring for, nourishing, and empathizing, and the word *anthropos*, which is the Greek word to signify all human beings. What Prometheus loved was our potential. The gift of fire completed the creation of humans.

Philanthropia, loving what it is to be human, came to be associated with service and generosity in ancient Greece, and the term was often used to describe political leaders during times of peace.[3] It was also connected with the highest ideals of civilization and culture. Philanthropic gifts served to strengthen cultural ties and symbolize communal solidarity. The wealthy would take on the duty (either

---

3   Marty Sulek, "On the Classical Meaning of Philanthropia," *Nonprofit and Voluntary Sector Quarterly*, June 2010.

voluntarily or due to peer pressure) to subsidize the cost of theaters and cultural events such as dramatic festivals.[4]

Plato's writing gives us an idea of the philosophical conception of philanthropy in the fourth century BC. In his dramatic work *The Symposium*, Plato depicts a contest of speeches by notable individuals at a banquet, including the philosopher Socrates, the general and political figure Alcibiades, and the comic playwright Aristophanes. The speeches are all given in praise of Eros, the god of love and desire. In his speech, Aristophanes praises Eros as "the most philanthropic of gods, a helper of human beings as well as a physician dealing with an illness the healing of which would result in the greatest happiness for the human race." Elsewhere, in the *Euthyphro*, Plato has Socrates describe his own mission as a teacher as a philanthropic one. Eventually, members of Plato's Academy offered a formal definition of the term in their philosophical dictionary: "A state of well-educated habits stemming from love of humans. A state of being productive of benefit to humans. A state of grace. Mindfulness together with good works."[5]

In ancient Greece, philanthropy was also becoming more explicitly associated with financial gifts to charity. Greek subjects would address the emperors of Byzantium as "Your Philanthropy," and the term *philanthropy* itself was used to refer to the tax exemption emperors gave to charities like hospitals, orphanages, and schools. This practice is the root of the tax-exempt status of many modern charities.

All these definitions find modern echoes in our contemporary view of philanthropy. These various historical meanings—from the mythological archetype and the philosophical depiction of human

---

4   Sarah Bond, "Philanthropy in Ancient Times: Some Early Examples from the Mediter-
     ranean," SOFII History Project, April 2, 2011, https://sofii.org/article/philanthropy-
     in-ancient-times-some-early-examples-from-the-mediterranean#:~:text=The%20
     Greeks%20also%20adopted%20the,desire%20they%20imparted%20to%20men.

5   Sulek, "On the Classical Meaning of Philanthropia."

nature to the ideals of civic and political virtue—all point to the idea that philanthropy is inherent to the human condition. This was Adam Smith's position. Smith may be more well known as the economist who gave us our contemporary image of capitalism, guided by the invisible hand of the marketplace, but you can also look at his work as a study in humanity with the premise that capitalism is the ultimate self-regulating economic system in relation to our nature. That said, a piece of this puzzle is still missing. Why do nonprofits emerge from capitalism? While it has something to do with our human nature, the organization of a nonprofit into a powerful economic unit that lacks owners but can compete for wealth in the economy is a strange occurrence in capitalism when you think about it.

CHAPTER 2

The Nonprofit in American Society

Democratic capitalism may be the best organization of human civilization that we've achieved in our history as a species. Democracy recognizes the inherent equality of all humans and enables the dream that anyone may seek and possibly achieve wealth, success, or happiness. Capitalism may be the most efficient means of advancement and maintenance of business and social relationships that is possible in relation to our human nature.

In modern American society, democratic capitalism is the playing field on which humans engage in production, trade, operations, business, relationships, and marriage. To what aim is capitalism? At its basest level, it is survival. But the aspiration of capitalists is more than survival; it is to amass enough wealth to meet all of one's needs. Those with few needs unmet are our most lucky, for they are the truly wealthy.

In the United States, our corporations and companies have one fiduciary direction—to generate as much profit as possible for shareholders. Our corporations and companies thrive in free market competition. This is the hallmark of capitalism: the singular goal to be more profitable, to amass treasure without end.

Such is the way of democratic capitalism. Yet within this system, nonprofits exist. And nonprofits don't merely exist. They flourish. In the United States, a significant portion of our economy is contained in nonprofit and charitable organizations. Nonprofits possess endowments and real estate holdings in the trillions of dollars, and many have existed for decades—some, for centuries. Consider that in 2019 the gross domestic product of the United States was approximately $21 trillion, while the net wealth of all nonprofit organizations filing tax returns with the Internal Revenue Services (IRS) for fiscal year 2019 was around $4.8 trillion.[6] Nonprofits are also job creators. In 2017, the nonprofit sector accounted for 10.2 percent of all private-sector jobs, according to the US Bureau of Labor Statistics, with 66.7 percent of such jobs being in healthcare and social assistance followed by 16.2 percent in educational services.[7]

Contrary to their name, nonprofits exist to make profit just like all business enterprises in democratic capitalism. The difference, however, is the *purpose* of the nonprofit. Nonprofits, in their very nature, are charitable. They must serve the public and make the community a better place from one generation to the next. Nonprofits can address societal discrepancies and injustices in a manner unlike any other, with a planning horizon that can be generations into the future. Nonprofits are particularly well suited to maintain community assets that are designed to feed our souls—such as libraries, museums, performance spaces, athletic facilities, theaters, parks, and gardens—not to mention the additional support of artists, athletes, and students to

6   See "Nonprofit Charitable and Other Tax-Exempt Organizations, Tax Year 2019," IRS. gov, https://www.irs.gov/pub/irs-pdf/p5331.pdf.

7   "How Many Nonprofits Are There in the US?" USAFACTS, November 16, 2023, https://usafacts.org/articles/how-many-nonprofits-are-there-in-the-us/.

fill such spaces with culture, history, music, arts, drama, competition, sport, athleticism, and education.

Consider Carnegie Hall in New York, the Schermerhorn in Nashville, the Gaillard Center in Charleston, or Disney Hall in Los Angeles. These spaces exist because of the work of philanthropists and nonprofits. Would Lincoln Center come alive without nonprofits like Jazz at Lincoln Center? Festivals like Spoleto USA, Lollapalooza, and the New Orleans Jazz & Heritage Festival are all presented by nonprofit organizations. Would it surprise you to learn that the International Olympic Committee, the guardian of the Olympic Games, is a nonprofit organization that was formed in 1894?

Churches and Religious Organizations

Nonprofits feed our souls in other ways. The United States was founded with the concept of religious tolerance and the freedom to worship. Churches and religious organizations formed some of the earliest nonprofit organizations in America. They exist by the generosity of their congregants and lack any owners in the corporate sense. In the US nonprofit sector, churches and religious organizations receive the largest share of charitable contributions. Of the $499 billion of charitable contributions made to nonprofits in 2022, $143 billion went to churches and religious organizations.[8] That represents close to one-third of all charitable giving in the United States. Most of these

---

8   "Giving USA: Total U.S. Charitable Giving Declined in 2022 to $499.33 Billion Following Two Years of Record Generosity," Lilly Family School of Philanthropy, IUPUI, June 20, 2023, https://philanthropy.iupui.edu/news-events/news/_news/2023/giving-usa-total-us-charitable-giving-declined-in-2022-to-49933-billion-following-two-years-of-record-generosity.html.

donations are made by individuals to the local church, synagogue, mosque, or temple where they regularly attend service.[9]

Religious faith has a great influence on giving. Religious people are more likely than the nonreligious to donate to charitable causes, and they give much more. Persons who attend religious services at least twice a month generally give to charity over four times as much as those who never go to religious services.[10] The giving of religious people is not just limited to their church—on the contrary, they are in general more philanthropic, providing support to other nonprofit sectors representing a diverse array of causes.

Schools and Educational Organizations

Nonprofits not only help us learn more about our religious and spiritual beliefs, but they also teach us in the arts, sciences, mathematics, and humanities. In 2020–21, among 5,916 postsecondary institutions that could process US federal student aid, 1,892, or 31 percent, were incorporated as nonprofit organizations.[11]

The number of notable institutions of higher education that have been created by philanthropists in the form of nonprofit organizations is impressive. The establishment of universities was a trend of philanthropists at the height of the age of industrialism.

- **Stanford University**. In 1885, Leland Stanford, former governor of California and railroad magnate, founded Stanford University in memory of his son, Leland Stanford Jr., who died

---

9   "The Ultimate List of Charitable Giving Statistics for 2023," Nonprofits Source, accessed February 23, 2024, https://nonprofitssource.com/online-giving-statistics/.

10   "Statistics on U.S. Generosity," Philanthropy Roundtable, accessed March 7, 2024, https://www.philanthropyroundtable.org/almanac/statistics-on-u-s-generosity/.

11   National Center for Education Statistics, August 2023, https://nces.ed.gov/programs/coe/indicator/cuc/financial-aid-sources.

as a teenager of typhoid fever. Stanford's initial gift included land and funds to establish the university. It's estimated that he donated approximately $40 million to the university.

- **Carnegie Mellon University**. Andrew Carnegie, the Scottish American industrialist and philanthropist, founded Carnegie Institute of Technology in 1900 with a gift of $2 million. It later merged with the Mellon Institute to become Carnegie Mellon in 1967.

- **Vanderbilt University**. Cornelius Vanderbilt, a prominent industrialist and shipping magnate, endowed $1 million in 1873 to establish Vanderbilt University in Nashville, Tennessee.

- **University of Chicago**. The University of Chicago was founded in 1890 with a substantial gift from John D. Rockefeller, one of America's wealthiest individuals at the time. It is estimated that he donated $35 million between 1892 and 1910 to the school.

- **Duke University**. Duke University was established in 1924 with a significant endowment from James Buchanan Duke, a tobacco and energy magnate. Duke's gift enabled the transformation of Trinity College into Duke University. His contributions are estimated to have been around $40 million during his lifetime.

- **Johns Hopkins University**. Johns Hopkins University was founded in 1876 through a planned gift of Johns Hopkins, a Baltimore merchant and investor. Hopkins left $7 million in his will to establish the university and the Johns Hopkins Hospital, which together formed the cornerstone of the Johns Hopkins Institutions.

Hospitals and Healthcare Providers

In the healthcare sector, the percentage of hospitals skews even greater toward nonprofit organizations than that seen in higher education. Of the 6,120 hospitals reported in existence in the United States in 2022, 2,987, or 48 percent, were nonprofit community hospitals.[12] Other nonprofit organizations like the Red Cross, Doctors Without Borders, and Operation Smile have spread across the world to increase access to modern healthcare treatments on a massive scale.

Additionally, nonprofit healthcare organizations engage in significant community benefit activities aimed at improving population health, addressing social determinants of health, and promoting community well-being. According to the American Hospital Association, in 2019 nonprofit hospitals invested over $110 billion in community benefit programs, including health education, disease prevention, community health initiatives, and subsidized healthcare services.[13]

How We Got Here

In the United States, the modern tax-exempt sector finds its roots in the period before the formation of the republic. Without an established government, early American colonists formed charitable and "voluntary" associations—including hospitals, orphanages, and fire departments—to address a variety of problems and social ills.[14]

---

12   "Fast Facts on US Hospitals, 2024," American Hospital Association, accessed February 23, 2024, https://www.aha.org/statistics/fast-facts-us-hospitals.

13   "Results from 2019 Tax-Exempt Hospitals' Schedule H Community Benefit Reports," American Hospital Association, June 2022, https://www.aha.org/system/files/media/file/2022/06/aha-2019-schedule-h-reporting.pdf.

14   Paul Arnsberger, Melissa Ludlum, Margaret Riley, and Mark Stanton; "A History of the Tax-Exempt Sector: An SOI Perspective"; *Statistics of Income Bulletin; Winter 2008;* https://www.irs.gov/pub/irs-soi/tehistory.pdf.

Centuries later, these types of voluntary organizations continue to thrive in the form of our contemporary nonprofit organizations.

Alexis de Tocqueville, a French diplomat and historian, is best known for observing and writing about living standards and social conditions of individuals in the early days of the United States. In 1831, de Tocqueville wrote the following:

> Americans of all ages, conditions, and dispositions con-
> stantly unite together. Not only do they have commercial
> and industrial associations to which all belong but also a
> thousand other kinds, religious, moral, serious, futile …
> Americans group together to hold fetes, found seminaries,
> build inns, construct churches, distribute books …They
> establish prisons, schools by the same method … I have
> frequently admired the endless skill with which the inhabit-
> ants of the United States manage to set a common aim to
> the efforts of a great number of men and to persuade them
> to pursue it voluntarily.[15]

Many of the Founding Fathers sought to dedicate their wealth back to their home communities through lifetime and planned gifts. They were looking to set an example for an emerging nation that was seeking an identity as a society. The period of the late 1700s is known now as the Age of Enlightenment, where individuals pursued the ideals of classical Greece, including the reemergence of philan-thropy as a central virtue of community and democratic society. To be "enlightened" meant, among other things, to be mindful of the needs of society and your fellow human.

---

15   Alexis de Tocqueville, *Democracy in America* (2003), Penguin Books, London, England, p. 596.

George Washington lived by the credo "never let an indigent person ask without receiving something if you have the means."[16] His lifelong support for charitable causes is reflected in the hundreds of expenditures recorded in his ledgers for "charity."[17] Even as the Revolutionary War was starting, he insisted on maintaining his assistance of the poor, writing to his cousin and Mount Vernon farm manager Lund Washington in November 1775, "Let the Hospitality of the House, with respect to the Poor, be kept up; Let no one go hungry away … and I have no objection to your giving my money in Charity to the amount of Forty or Fifty pounds a year, when you think it well bestowed. What I mean by having no objection, is, that it is my desire that it should be done."[18]

Later in life, Washington donated to schools, churches, orphanages, and charities for the needy such as the Alexandria Poor Relief Committee. He strongly believed in the value of education. This support extended to higher education, including most notably a major gift to Washington and Lee University that he made three years before his death. According to the university, this gift lives on to this day. The university estimates that the original grant from Washington underwrites eleven dollars of each student's tuition.

Another founder, Benjamin Franklin, made significant charitable contributions to the city of Philadelphia in order to establish

---

16   "From George Washington to George Washington Parke Custis, November 15, 1796," Founders Online, National Archives, last modified Aug. 3, 2021, http://founders. archives.gov/documents/Washington/99-01-02-00007. The information in the following paragraphs draws from Adrina Garbooshian-Huggins, "George Washington and Charity," Washington Papers, September 3, 2021, https://washingtonpapers. org/george-washington-and-charity/.

17   See, for example, General Ledger A, January 16, 1764, http://financial.gwpapers. org/?q=content/ledger-1750-1772-pg175.

18   "From George Washington to Lund Washington, 26 November 1775," Founders Online, National Archives, last modified August 4, 2021, https://founders.archives. gov/documents/Washington/03-02-02-0396.

its first public library, first hospital, first volunteer fire department, and even its first streetlight. His Academy of Philadelphia became the University of Pennsylvania in 1750.[19] Less than a year before his death on April 17, 1790, Benjamin Franklin added a codicil to his will whereby he bequeathed £1,000, the equivalent of $4,000, to each of the cities of Boston and Philadelphia. He restricted the expenditure of the principal of the gift through charitable trusts to run for two hundred years. The principal was not to be spent, but the income arising therefrom was expendable in support of trade schools and public works. The funds for his trusts were accumulated from his salary as governor of Pennsylvania from 1785 to 1788, a move informed by the belief that public servants should not be paid. It was a rule he had tried unsuccessfully to include in the Constitution.[20]

At the end of the first hundred years, Franklin's Boston endowment had grown to roughly $391,000. Over the following hundred years, proceeds of the endowment went to support public works in Boston, including $322,490 to establish the Benjamin Franklin Institute of Technology in the early 1900s. At the end of two hundred years, in 1990, the two endowments together were worth nearly $6,500,000. Consider the power of Franklin's philanthropic model, based on compound growth of restricted principal untouched for over two centuries. These two city trusts continue to fund public works and help thousands of young people achieve their academic dreams with scholarships.

---

19   Christopher Levenick, "Benjamin Franklin," Philanthropy Roundtable, accessed February 9, 2024, https://www.philanthropyroundtable.org/hall-of-fame/benjamin-franklin/.

20   Fox Butterfield, "From Ben Franklin, a Gift That's Worth Two Fights," *New York Times*, *April 21, 1990,* https://www.nytimes.com/1990/04/21/us/from-ben-franklin-a-gift-that-s-worth-two-fights.html.

The Modern American Nonprofit

The early associations of *people for a common good* observed by de Tocqueville, which were prevalent in colonial America, have evolved considerably in scope and structure to what we see currently in the United States. Today, for eligibility as a tax-exempt organization under Internal Revenue Code section 501(c)(3), the IRS recognizes nonprofits as one of two possible types. A 501(c)(3) organization is either a *public charity* or a *private foundation*.

A public charity is a nonprofit that receives its financial support, broadly, from the general public. A public charity typically has a self-perpetuating board of directors, the directors being unrelated to one another by blood, business, or marriage. Examples of public charities include the Boys and Girls Club, Big Brothers Big Sisters, the Red Cross, YMCAs, St. Jude's Children's Research Hospital, Save the Children, and the Society for the Prevention of Cruelty to Animals. Churches, hospitals, and universities also typically fall into the category of public charities.

By contrast, a private foundation is a nonprofit that is funded and controlled by a company or a family, with a board of directors that is handpicked by such company or family. Private foundations are grant-making vehicles for philanthropists and are often used by family offices as the entity with responsibility to manage and conduct the family's philanthropic activities. Private foundations are typically funded with significant income-generating investments and usually have endowments. Examples of private foundations include the Bill & Melinda Gates Foundation and the Home Depot Foundation.

Both types of nonprofits follow a charitable purpose, but the public charity is the more prevalent type of nonprofit, maintaining public-facing programs and operations that impact segments of the population. Private foundations are often grant-making organizations, typically funding public charities.

The lessons of this handbook apply to both types of organizations.

Trendlines

Let's look at the trends in philanthropy over the last forty years. The nonprofit sector appears to be experiencing an incredible trajectory of growth in terms of number of charities in existence, their annual revenue, and their net worth.

In 1985, the IRS recognized the existence of approximately 310,000 public charities. At that time, it required only 106,449 of these nonprofits to file a Form 990 tax return.[21] Those filers reported revenues of $268.4 billion. In terms of assets, the net worth of these organizations was reported at $237.2 billion.

By 2004, we see a jump to almost 900,000 IRS-recognized public charities. Of that number, 276,119 were required to file the Form 990 tax return.[22] These organizations reported nearly $1.2 trillion in revenue and a net worth just in excess of $1.2 trillion.

By 2019, there were 1,386,744 nonprofits recognized by the IRS, with 304,231 filing the Form 990 tax return.[23] These nonprofits reported revenues of $2.4 trillion and net assets worth $2.9 trillion.

---

21 Cecilia Hilgert and Susan J. Mahler, "Nonprofit Charitable Organizations, 1985," *Statistics of Income Bulletin, Fall 1989, Volume 9, Number 2, pp. 53–65*, https://www.irs.gov/pub/irs-soi/85npco.pdf.

22 Arnsberger et al., "A History of the Tax-Exempt Sector: An SOI Perspective."

23 See "Nonprofit Charitable and Other Tax-Exempt Organizations, Tax Year 2019," IRS. gov, https://www.irs.gov/pub/irs-pdf/p5331.pdf.

NONPROFITS & IRS FORM 990S

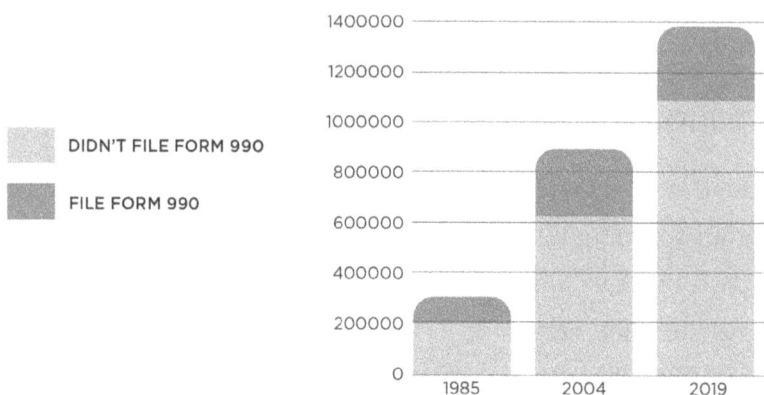

In terms of these trends, for the period from 1985 to 2019, the number of nonprofits filing the Form 990 increased by 200 percent. If you think about it, you are only required to file the Form 990 if you are a nonprofit with any material revenue or assets. Over the years, small nonprofits had alternate filing methods, like e-postcards, or for some periods were just not required to file. These are the really small nonprofits, often start-ups. If you look at the growth in total public charities regardless of size, you see that the total number of nonprofits from 1985 to 2019 increased by 450 percent. That signals to me a concurrent increase in the number of start-up nonprofits that failed to launch during the last forty years. It also tells me that the current market is teeming with poor-performing nonprofits, with the barrier to entry too low.

If you look at the increase in annual revenue across the nonprofit sector by comparing data from 1985 to 2019, you will see that revenue reported on the Form 990 reflected an increase of almost 1,000 percent (from $268.4 billion in 1985 to $2.4 trillion in 2019). Let's compare nonprofit sector revenue against the US gross domestic product (GDP) for the same two years. In 1985, the US GDP was $4.3 billion, and in 2019 it was $21 billion. That is an increase of 500 percent. So, comparing the year 1985 to the year 2019, reported revenue of nonprofits grew at twice the rate of growth of US GDP over the same period.

Percent of Change to Net Worth, Revenue & Total Expenses Compared to GDP
1985-2019

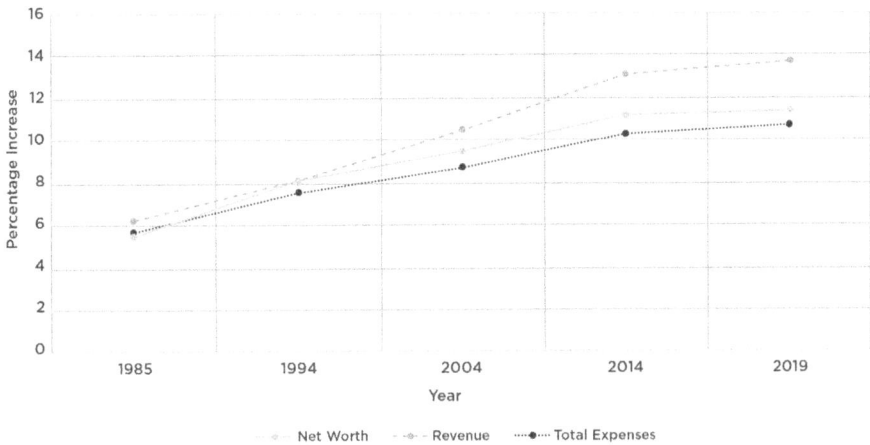

It's important to note that the growth in GDP was not steady over the entire period. The United States experienced a major economic recession in 2008–09 due to the subprime mortgage crisis, which led to a significant short-term decline in GDP. However, the economy began to recover in 2010 and continued to grow steadily for the remainder of the period. Over that same period, the value of the charitable asset base of all nonprofit organizations filing Form 990 expanded at an even higher rate. From 1985 to 2019, the net worth of public charities reporting on Form 990 increased by approximately 1,900 percent, resulting in reported net worth in 2019 across the nonprofit sector of $4.8 trillion.

Percent Increases

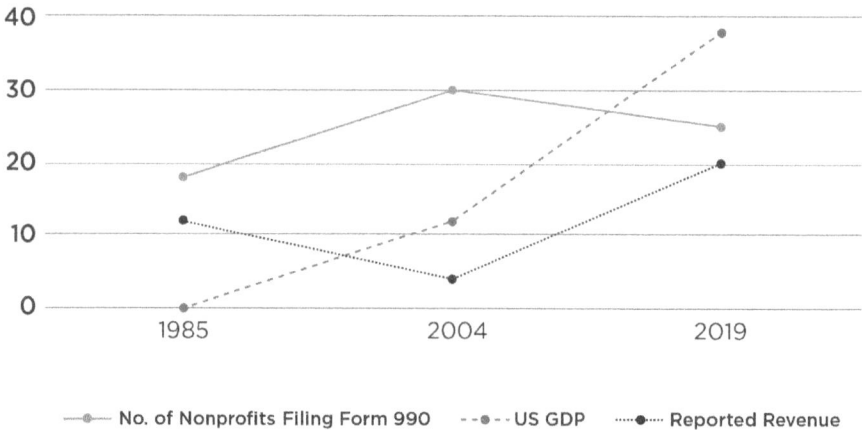

Whether this increase in asset bases of nonprofit organizations is a result of increased philanthropy and charitable giving, increasingly sophisticated investment of endowment funds, and/or some combination of other factors, it's encouraging to see this trendline over the last forty-plus years in the United States.

Now that you have a frame of reference, consider the generational transfer of wealth from aging baby boomers to charity currently projected to be $12 trillion in the next twenty years. That generation has the ability to quadruple the $4.8 trillion net worth of the entire nonprofit sector in two decades. If all $17 trillion were contained in permanently restricted endowments subject to a 3 percent distribution requirement, that would generate $510 billion each year thereafter for use by nonprofits. In 2023, the United States GDP was $27 billion. While I'm sure that by 2043 the US GDP could top $60 billion, my point is that the financial output of the nonprofit sector is outpacing the rate of growth of US GDP. And in the next twenty years, we will see a supercharging of wealth in nonprofits.

Given the history and these numbers, you can't claim that non-profits are an anomaly in democratic capitalism. But still, this leaves the question unanswered: *Why?*

CHAPTER 3

Why Do Nonprofits Exist within Capitalism?

We can account for the history of philanthropy from ancient Greece to the contemporary United States, but we still haven't answered our question: *Why* do nonprofits exist at all in capitalism? Consider the following:

- In the singular drive for "profit," does something get lost?

- Do economic, health, and educational gaps and disparities emerge in our communities as a by-product of capitalism?

- Are nonprofits the means to fill the gaps and address inefficiencies and disparities?

- Do nonprofits create or advance societal values that bind communities together?

The philanthropist will likely believe that there is a correlation between the presence of the nonprofit sector within a democratic capitalistic society and the overall success of such society. To a philanthropist, success is measured from a global humanistic perspective.

This includes *subjective measures* such as quality of life, low incidence of deaths by despair, or percentage of population with accessibility to quality, affordable healthcare. It also includes *objective measures* such as wage growth, currency value, or market performance. In an ideal economy, is there a perfect balance of nonprofit to for-profit businesses that promotes the overall success of democratic capitalism?

Nonprofits have an incredible ability to be efficient and to have their performance measured in terms of dollars delivered to mission versus administrative overhead and expense. A well-performing nonprofit might spend 15–25 percent of its budget for administration costs and the remainder to deploy its programs. The US federal government currently spends a good bit more on its administrative overhead. Given their efficiencies and public orientation, nonprofit organizations generally lessen the burdens of government and allow individuals to address their community problems on their own.

The Relationship of the Philanthropist and the Nonprofit

As I think about the existence of the nonprofit organization in a democratic capitalist society, I can't help but have an image of nonprofits as social therapeutics within a free marketplace, designed to improve the lives of people, with such therapeutics being legally deployed by responsible citizens, otherwise known herein as philanthropists. What strikes me is that one of the key tasks of the philanthropist within capitalism is to compete with individuals and for-profits that also desire to amass as much wealth as possible. In doing so, philanthropists can work to restrict asset bases through endowments, trusts, and sophisticated giving arrangements, with the objective to protect those in need and those who are our most vulnerable. These restrictions are designed to exist beyond the life of the philanthropist and, in theory, may continue in perpetuity.

Look back to the example of Benjamin Franklin's Philadelphia and Boston endowments. Franklin understood that to really benefit each city, he needed to set aside a portion of his money after death and sequester it away from the marketplace. In doing so, he required that only the income, and never the principal, of each endowment was to be spent. In other words, his actions more than two hundred years ago are precisely what we now recognize as a central plank of philanthropy: making a planned gift into an endowment. For this money to have a lasting impact, the principal needed to be protected from disappearing into the marketplace.

Nonprofits play a critical role in relation to philanthropists and the execution of our philanthropic plans. Nonprofits are the vehicles into which philanthropists amass wealth restricted for the charitable mission to advance and improve humanity. Nonprofits are the organizations that protect and maintain these endowments in perpetuity. Their boards and staff execute on your mission long after you are gone.

So, this is the key. In democratic capitalism, philanthropists compete with for-profit businesses and individuals to amass wealth, which they place in nonprofits. In doing so, philanthropists redirect a portion of our economy into a public purpose as opposed to a purpose singularly driven for profit at the cost of all other things, including people. It is this balance, this competition, that helps build communities and is the critical difference in quality and purpose of life for each of us.

If you are to be a philanthropist, this is your strategic vision for deployment of your philanthropic plan. This is a central role you play in society.

Consider this proverb: When is the best time to plant a tree? Twenty years ago. When is the next best time to plant a tree? Today.

The proverb provokes the image of an old man or woman in his or her elder years planting a young tree sapling. They know they will never live long enough to enjoy its shade in the summer months, scale its branches, watch birds nest year after year, and see its roots extend far underground and its branches reach outward, strong and uplifting. Philanthropists are those individuals who are planting trees that will blossom and thrive long after they are gone. Nonprofits are our trees filling the economic landscape.

When I think in these terms, my imagination won't let me escape the idea of philanthropists becoming some form of nonprofit Johnny Appleseed, planting trees of economic hope in our capitalist landscape. Over time, if they are well cared for, if they acquire the ability to amass institutional knowledge and gain organizational intelligence, and if they increase their purchasing power from one generation to the next, then one day we might see a forest of such trees.

Philanthropy as a Basis for Ethics in Capitalist Society

Capitalism is not static. Economies are in constant flux. The ripples are widespread, with unintended consequences, making the rich poor and the poor rich over and over again. This has always been the case. Advancements in *technology*, using that term very broadly, often create the more significant disruptions in our economy that our laws, culture, and society just aren't ready to process. It's in these periods where the gaps, disparities, and injustices that exist in democratic capitalism become more pronounced. Sometimes the disparities arise as a result of the advancement. Other times the advancements deepen or reveal preexisting conditions. It's a complex problem. Advancements also improve the human condition. Our leaps in technology represent the ever-growing accumulation of knowledge. Improvement of the human condition is a goal that philanthropists share.

In capitalism, this is another area where I believe philanthropy and nonprofits come into play. I believe philanthropy plays a role in the healing of societal ills resulting from or revealed by technological advancements. Let's look at another case study.

An example of a leap for which our society was not prepared was the creation of the first immortal human cell line, known as the "HeLa cell." The breadth of biomedical discoveries and life-saving healthcare treatments attributed to the HeLa cell is staggering—from chromosome counting and genome mapping to the development of modern vaccines. This cell line was used to lay the groundwork to create the polio vaccine in the 1950s; used to determine how radiation affects the body, thereby creating a standard for X-rays; used to develop a variety of cancer treatments; used to advance cell imaging; and used to create in vitro fertilization. The first human cells sent to space were HeLa cells. Visit almost any cell culture lab today, and you will find millions, if not billions, of frozen HeLa cells.

When we talk about the great advancements in healthcare and medical treatment with which humans are now endowed as a result of the HeLa cell, we cannot forget that this is a human cell. It came from a real person. In 1951, Mrs. Henrietta Lacks, a thirty-one-year-old African American woman, died from an aggressive form of cervical cancer, only ten months after first seeking treatment at Johns Hopkins Hospital. During her treatment at the hospital, samples of cancerous tissue were taken from her cervix and then used in widespread research thereafter, including for significant and varied commercial, money-making purposes. The HeLa cell was named after the first two letters of Henrietta Lacks's first and last name.

Neither Mrs. Lacks nor her family gave permission for her cells to be taken. An article in *Ebony* magazine in 1976 featured a quote from her husband. He said, "All I remember is that she had this disease, and right after she died they called me in the office wanting to get my permission to take a sample of some kind. I decided not to let them."[24]

At the time, it was standard to take tumor cells for research without consent. But eventually, Henrietta Lacks's family became understandably upset. The book *The Immortal Life of Henrietta Lacks*, written by Rebecca Skloot, is a close look into the effects upon the family of Henrietta Lacks, the confusion, and the negative impacts, including the general public becoming aware of significant personal information regarding Mrs. Lacks and her family. Notwithstanding the widespread commercial research that arose from HeLa cells, her family was neither compensated nor recognized for it for decades.

Consider the issue of white physicians claiming ownership over a young Black woman's cells. Ownership of actual pieces of her body … to this day.

At the time of Mrs. Lacks's death in 1951, when Jim Crow laws were still the norm throughout many parts of the United States, our society had yet to consider the ownership of tissue samples taken by a doctor, informed consent of patients in a treatment setting, and issues related to individual privacy and confidentiality arising in connection with healthcare treatment. It wasn't until 1991 that the United States adopted the Common Rule requiring informed consent from individuals for tissue donations. It wasn't until 1996 that the United States enacted the Health Insurance Portability and Accountability Act, also known as HIPAA, thereby adopting the first widespread

---

24   "The Miracle of 'HeLa," *Ebony, June 1976, pp. 93–98.*

rules regarding privacy of individuals' healthcare information. These changes in the law, which seem like basic rights to a person today, occurred almost a half century after Mrs. Lacks passed away. Consider Mrs. Lacks's human rights in 1950 versus what they might be today … or what they might be seventy-five years from now.

If we look back, philanthropists and nonprofits together played a meaningful role during the second half of the twentieth century to advocate for patient rights and be a catalyst for the enactment of the Common Rule and HIPAA in the 1990s.

By the 1960s, advocates such as Ruth Ravich, who helped establish the Society for Healthcare Consumer Advocacy and the first Patient Representative Department at Mount Sinai Hospital, began to demand attention to these issues. In 1970, the Institute of Medicine was established to pursue objective and scientifically balanced answers to difficult questions of societal importance related to the delivery and accessibility of healthcare, as well as ethical considerations arising in connection with human subject research. In 1972, the American Hospital Association adopted its first patient bill of rights into the accreditation standards for hospitals.[25]

Here's another example: In 1990, Dr. Harold P. Freeman, a surgical oncologist at Harlem Hospital, developed the concept of "patient navigation" to lower barriers to cancer screening, diagnosis, treatment, and supportive care. Over time, Dr. Freeman's program evolved to consider the movement of an individual across the entire healthcare continuum from prevention, detection, diagnosis, and treatment to end-of-life care. At the National Institutes of Health, the Center to Reduce Cancer Health Disparities was created in 2001

---

25 Elisabeth Schuler, "History and Trends in the Field of Healthcare Advocacy," *CSA Journal 85(4), 2021,* https://aphadvocates.org/assets/History-Trends-CSA-Schuler-12.21.pdf.

in response to meaningful data from Dr. Freeman's programs. As evidence accrued in support of his findings, Congress passed the Patient Navigator Outreach and Chronic Disease Prevention Act in 2005, which authorized $25 million over the next five years to develop community-based navigation programs. Consider what Mrs. Lacks's treatment and end-of-life experience might have been like today as a result of nonprofit advocacy since the 1950s.

When you think about the impact to population health, emergent technology often juxtaposes miraculous cures against issues related to accessibility of care. Consider that in 2023, medical technology and pharmaceuticals made up almost 25 percent of the nearly three hundred thousand patent applications filed in the United States.[26] Clearly, healthcare technology dominates innovation in the United States, and that is a good thing. But when you think about it, there is a reason that of the 6,120 hospitals in the United States, 48 percent are nonprofit community hospitals.[27] Consider the landscape of healthcare in the United States, where almost half our hospitals are nonprofits.

Technology advances the human condition in the long haul. Go into any intensive care unit or emergency room in the United States, and you will see it before your eyes. But technology also has a downside. It can take years, even decades, before society and our lawmakers begin to comprehend the implications of such advancements to our communities. In the interim, the lack of comprehensive legal frameworks can result in inequitable access to emerging technologies, leading to disparities in terms of economic opportunities,

---

26 Veera Korhonen, "Number of Patent Applications in the United States in 2020, by Top Fields of Technology," Statista, June 2, 2023, https://www.statista.com/statistics/256734/percentage-of-patent-applications-in-the-us-by-fields-of-technology/.

27 "Fast Facts on US Hospitals, 2024," https://www.aha.org/statistics/fast-facts-us-hospitals.

education, healthcare, and overall societal development. Emerging technologies can be exploited or misused, leaving society and individuals, like Mrs. Lacks and her family, vulnerable to potential harms.

Any major technological leap will cause significant social and economic disruptions. This includes not just leaps in realms such as advanced computing or biotechnology that we might think of today but also going back in time to the steam engine, the printing press, the discovery of bronze, even the emergence of farming. During periods of rapid technological advancement, again using the word *technology* in the broadest sense possible, the world experiences upheaval for some time, until everything evens out and we're able to reflect on the changes in retrospect. Once that happens, those reflections start to crystallize into new sets of values and, hopefully, laws.

It can take a while for laws to catch up with technology—just look at the many years of exploitation and poor treatment of workers, including children, that occurred during the Industrial Revolution before protections were finally put in place. Remember the stories of Charles Dickens, who often depicted the exploitation of children in nineteenth-century Britain—think of *Oliver Twist*, *David Copperfield*, or the orphan Pip in *Great Expectations*. It took the emergence of labor unions, such as the Federal Society of Journeymen Cordwainers (shoemakers) in 1794, the Mechanics' Union of Trade Associations in 1827, and the International Typographical Union in 1852, for enough voices to start to effect legal change.[28] It shouldn't surprise you that labor unions are typically nonprofit organizations. Even today, look at the difficulty with which our own Congress struggles to come to terms with the digital revolution. As deepfakes sweep across our country, as of this writing only nine states have laws that address the ill effects of

---

28   "Labor Movement," History.com, March 30, 2020, https://www.history.com/topics/19th-century/labor.

this technology. Congress itself has done nothing, notwithstanding the effects to our elections, institutions, and civility. What nonprofits will emerge to help us come to terms with the societal implications of these advancements in technology?

As we consider the many roles of the philanthropist in society, we can also see a responsibility to push forward these ethical reflections and conversations, to speak loudly and insist that new protections and values be put in place, and to respond with empathy and fund social cures to mend these ills. Philanthropists run ahead of market and governmental reforms to heal the injustices and imbalances of technological upheavals. Philanthropy provides a basis for the advancement of ethics in democratic capitalist societies, unhindered by politics or time and able to respond with compassion to disruptive economic change.

Might another role of the philanthropist be to deploy restricted asset bases in a manner that drives conversations about ethics and values in our homes and public spaces to address the problems of the day?

Might it also be that nonprofits are the champions of philanthropists, carrying the torch from one generation to the next?

Our Nonprofit Champions

To answer the question of why nonprofits exist in capitalist democracies, we've looked at the history of philanthropy from ancient Greece to the United States. We've seen the data points and the trendlines in the United States over the last forty years. We know a part of the answer lies within us. Philanthropy is in our nature. It is the balancing force in an economic system whose sole objective is profit. We know that the hallmark of capitalism is change, largely the result of emerging technology that disrupts not just the marketplace but communities and people. The Prometheus archetype hints at the balance between technology and philanthropy. Whether through technology or charity, the urge to advance and improve the human condition is a form of love of humankind—it is the *philos anthropos*. Philanthropy helps us evaluate the effects of disruptive technology on our communities and enables us to respond with compassion, ultimately culminating in our drive to manifest ethics and laws in society.

New technologies continue to raise complex ethical dilemmas for which there may not be any clear legal guidance. Issues related to artificial intelligence, genetic engineering, energy, and robotics in the near future will present challenges in terms of accountability, liability, and the potential impact on human rights and societal values like we've never seen before. There will be greater demand upon our churches, schools, healthcare providers, and arts organizations to help us understand and respond to this ever-changing world. By having the foresight to recognize and meet these challenges, philanthropy can help us to navigate the complexities of emerging technologies while pursuing the protection of individuals, promoting innovation, and fostering responsible development.

We also have foresight to see our own death. That's why we plan gifts to charity. Each of us may be equipped to see the challenges that exist in our world today, but we also know that there will be a tomorrow when we won't be here anymore. Nonprofits are our champions in capitalism. They are partners in our philanthropic plans.

Philanthropists play many roles in this world. We restrict funds and assets in our economy to be dedicated forever toward a charitable mission. We direct that mission to heal any ill effects from capitalism, thereby raising the quality of life of everyone in our society. We carry conversations across generations to evaluate and seek improvement within our world. We need nonprofits to fulfill our many roles as philanthropists. After we are gone, nonprofits carry forward our endowments, not just of money but of knowledge and mission. Nonprofits are the vehicles through which philanthropists may communicate with each other across generations.

In our history, we see nonprofits rising to meet the challenges of each generation. Nonprofits can execute on your mission long after you are gone. They carry our legacy forward. They manage our accumulated wealth forever into the future for the betterment of humankind. This is really why nonprofits exist. This is their role in capitalism and in relation to us.

We've seen the definition of philanthropy evolve over time, from its origin with Aeschylus to the modern American context. I'd like to add one new element to the definition:

Philanthropy is the output of philanthropists and nonprofits working together collaboratively.

This expands the definition of philanthropy to not just include individual contributions to the public good but also to encompass the relationship, interplay, and common mission of philanthropy's two central players: the philanthropist and the nonprofit organization.

Our success as philanthropists depends not only on our ability to live in the philanthropic way and use our empathy, ethics, and foresight to seek cures for societal ills but also on how well we pick and support our nonprofit champions. How can we practice living in the philanthropic way, to cultivate the philanthropist within? Which nonprofits will reflect our own personal mission? Which ones will go the distance? How might we engage a nonprofit, legally, to ensure that it will fulfill our philanthropic plan? Let's explore these questions further.

PART 2

Living Philanthropically

Cultivate the habit of giving. Generosity brings happiness at every stage of its expression. We experience joy in forming the intention to be generous, joy in the actual act of giving, and joy in remembering the act of generosity.

—GAUTAMA BUDDHA

CHAPTER 4

Philanthropy as a Form of Self-Improvement

I suspect it was a cold evening on February 23, 1905, when Paul Harris called together a meeting of three friends in downtown Chicago. They met at Gustave Loehr's office in the Unity Building on Dearborn Street. Loehr was a mining engineer and freemason. They were joined by Silvester Schiele, a coal merchant, and Hiram E. Shorey, a tailor. Paul was an attorney. Paul wanted to start a club that would foster fellowship in the business community. This diverse group of businessmen chose the name "Rotary" due to their initial practice to rotate meetings among each other's offices.

Born on April 19, 1868, in Wisconsin, Paul moved to Wallingford, Vermont, at the age of three to be raised by his grandparents. In the foreword to his autobiography, *My Road to Rotary*, he credits the friendliness and tolerance he found in Vermont as his inspiration for the creation of Rotary.

Paul was an eclectic person who had a love for travel and was open to new experiences. After graduating law school in 1891, he gave himself five years to see as much of the world as possible before settling down and hanging out his shingle. "During that time, he traveled widely, supporting himself with a great variety of jobs. He worked as a reporter in San Francisco, a teacher at a business college in Los Angeles, a cowboy in Colorado, a desk clerk in Jacksonville, Florida, a tender of cattle on a freighter to England, and as a traveling salesman for a granite company, covering both the U.S. and Europe."[29]

But on that cold February night, Paul called his three friends together to discuss his idea that they might find in Chicago the kind of warm, friendly spirit Paul had known in Vermont where he'd grown up. Over the next five years, their club grew so large they had to abandon the rotation of gatherings and pick one spot to meet. It didn't stop there. The movement spread like wildfire as Rotary clubs were formed in other US cities and beyond. The next four Rotary Clubs were organized in San Francisco, then Oakland, Seattle, and Los Angeles, followed shortly thereafter by clubs in Dublin, London, and Winnipeg.

The mission of Rotary is to "provide service to others, promote integrity, and advance world understanding, goodwill, and peace through [the] fellowship of business, professional, and community leaders." Today, the widespread network of Rotary Clubs around the world sponsors programs focusing on education, fighting disease, providing clean water, and growing local economies such as the following:

- The Global Grants program, providing funds for large-scale projects that address community needs around the world

- The Youth Exchange program, promoting cultural exchange and understanding among young people from different countries

---

29 "The Boys of 1905: A History of Rotary International," Santa Rosa Sunrise Rotary, accessed February 7, 2024, https://portal.clubrunner.ca/4124/stories/the-boys-of-1905-a-history-of-rotary-international.

- The Peace Fellowship program, providing funds for graduate-level studies in peace and conflict resolution

- PolioPlus, working to eradicate polio worldwide

When the National Association of Rotary Clubs held its first convention in 1910, the members elected Paul as the inaugural president. After his term ended, and as the organization's only president emeritus, Paul continued to travel extensively, promoting the spread of Rotary both in the United States and abroad. Now, more than a hundred years later, there are over forty-six thousand member clubs worldwide, with a membership of 1.4 million individuals, known as Rotarians.[30]

It's an interesting case study to see this philanthropic movement emerge in Chicago at the beginning of the 1900s and achieve global scope, influence, and scale in membership and operations in just under a century. In many ways, it might be the first nonprofit organization to achieve global prominence in our history.

When you look at what makes a successful Rotary Club or Rotarian, you see a focus on empathy and foresight that is targeted to community service. An interesting by-product of this movement is its manifestation of an actual code of ethics—the Four-Way Test. The Four-Way Test is a guide for Rotarians to use in their personal and professional relationships. The test has been translated into more than a hundred languages. Rotarians recite it regularly at club meetings:

Of the things we think, say, or do—

1. Is it the TRUTH?

2. Is it FAIR to all concerned?

3. Will it build GOODWILL and BETTER FRIENDSHIPS?

---

30 "Who We Are," Rotary.org, accessed June 3, 2024, https://www.rotary.org/en/about-rotary.

4. Will it be BENEFICIAL to all concerned?

The Four-Way Test was originally created by Herbert J. Taylor. In 1932, the stockholders of Club Aluminum Company engaged Herbert to save the business from bankruptcy. Herbert's plan to turn the company around was to focus on the character, dependability, and service-mindedness of its personnel. He determined to be careful in the selection of employees and then help them, intentionally, to become better people as they progressed with the company.

To accomplish these goals, Herbert felt the company needed a simple measuring stick of ethics that everyone could memorize. The test shouldn't tell anyone what they must do but rather ask them whether their proposed actions were right or wrong. At Club Aluminum Company, all decisions thereafter—everything from advertising approval to relationships with vendors—were vetted through these four questions. Over time, it proved successful. Not only did the company experience a turnaround, these ethics began to infect the personal lives of Herbert and the staff.

Herbert wrote the following:

We have found that you cannot constantly apply the Four-Way Test to all your relations with others eight hours each day in business without getting into the habit of doing it in your home, social and community life. You thus become a better father, a better friend and a better citizen.[31]

In the 1940s, Herbert became an international director of Rotary, and he offered the Four-Way Test to the organization. It was quickly

31   Herbert J. Taylor, "Story of the Four-Way Test," quoted at Rotary5630.org, accessed June 3, 2024, https://rotary5630.org/history-of-the-four-way-test/#:~:text=We%20have%20found%20that%20you,friend%20and%20a%20better%20citizen.%E2%80%9D.

adopted. The Four-Way Test remains a central part of the permanent Rotary structure throughout the world and is held as a standard by which all Rotarian behavior may be measured.

When you consider Rotary as a global philanthropic movement, you see in its originator, Paul Harris, a thoughtful individual who spent some time considering how to capitalize on the "fellow-feeling" that Adam Smith heralded as the secret ingredient of capitalism in order to serve and draw the community together. In Herbert Taylor, you see a compassionate leader who was able to capture the Rotarian movement in a code of ethics. It's the honest pursuit of truth, grounded in empathy toward all the individuals in your community, that likely has resonated with so many individuals, drawing them to Rotary.

The other thing I find appealing about Rotary is that the movement has prioritized personal development. To be a Rotarian is to be dedicated to a form of self-improvement. It is the same to be a philanthropist.

Exercises to Align Yourself in the Philanthropic Way

In part 1 of this handbook, we discussed the role of the philanthropist to compete in a capitalist society for funds and assets, which can be restricted permanently in a nonprofit for a public purpose, thereby addressing inefficiencies, injustices, and disparities that can arise in democratic capitalism. In part 2, we will examine the personal qualities of the philanthropist and provide visual exercises intended to amplify these philanthropic qualities in you. Many of these exercises and thoughts are drawn from classical times when the cultivation of philanthropy was considered of paramount importance for the success of society. Many of these beliefs and practices continue to be exemplified in organizations like Rotary International. One of the many goals of this handbook is to help you become more in tune with your "fellow-feeling" as described by Adam Smith, your basic charitable nature, and to train that nature to make you a philanthropist.

Plato viewed philanthropy as an essential virtue of individuals and society as a whole. In *The Republic*, Plato describes the ideal society as one in which individuals are driven by a sense of duty to help others and promote the common good. In his view, philanthropy was not just about providing material assistance but also about cultivating a spirit of kindness and compassion toward others. Plato believed that philanthropy was beneficial not only to those who received help but also to those who gave it, as it helped them develop a sense of empathy and an appreciation for the interconnectedness of all human beings.

With this virtue in mind, consider yourself now a student of Plato's Academy. Let's begin to cultivate the skills you need to advance as a philanthropist. This handbook provides, among other things, three specific approaches to self-discipline and awareness intended to orient the mind toward the philanthropic way:

- Empathy
- Ethics of information and truth
- Foresight

As many ancient Greek philosophers believed, philanthropy is an approach to life that over time may provide an exceptional life experience for each of us. Philanthropy can be pursued intentionally, as a set of disciplines to exercise, based on love for humanity and a desire for *all of us* to succeed in perpetuity. It is a way that follows the lessons of the Promethean archetype, from which our language, society, and so many of our values, whether or not we're aware, are derived.

CHAPTER 5

The Discipline of Empathy

When you find yourself deeply invested in your empathic side, the causes to which you will be attracted will reflect your authentic self. Being empathic is about openness, creating an opening in oneself to receive the feelings of another. Empathy requires suspending your judgment and leaving behind your assumptions, fears, and stereotypes.

The American Psychological Association defines empathy as understanding another person's frame of reference rather than one's own, or "vicariously experiencing that person's feelings, perceptions, and thoughts."[32]

Greater Good Magazine from the University of California defines empathy this way: "The ability to sense other people's emotions, coupled with the ability to imagine what someone else might be thinking or feeling."[33]

---

32   "Empathy," *APA Dictionary of Psychology, accessed February 7, 2024,* https://dictionary.apa.org/empathy.

33   "What Is Empathy?," *Greater Good Magazine, accessed February 7, 2024,* https://greatergood.berkeley.edu/topic/empathy/definition#:~:text=Emotion%20researchers%20generally%20define%20empathy,might%20be%20thinking%20or%20feeling.

For the purposes of this handbook, you might come to think of the human condition as the lifetime movement across an axis, where on one end is ego, self, and narcissism and on the other end is empathy. Babies are born into the narcissist end of the axis. This is because they're inherently focused on survival in a world in which they depend on others to live.

In Plato's Academy, it might have been discoursed that life is about learning to move from ego toward increasing levels of empathy for others. For philanthropists, this is a basic tenet of their human experience and can be achieved with a conscious pursuit of self-improvement.

Provided here are activities that have the potential to expand your empathy in a philanthropic orientation. Let's be clear—these activities are really about self-care. Some of you are likely doing some or all of these activities currently. You don't have to go overboard. The point is to be mindful and consider the empathic qualities inherent in these activities when you are engaged in them. Remember the definition of philanthropy from Plato's Academy—"Mindfulness together with good works."

Practice Gratitude

The benefits of practicing gratitude, of *giving thanks*, are numerous: "People who regularly practice gratitude by taking time to notice and reflect upon the things for which they're thankful experience more positive emotions, feel more alive, sleep better, express more compassion and kindness, and even have stronger immune systems."[34]

---

34   Derrick Carpenter, "The Science behind Gratitude (and How It Can Change Your Life)," The Upside, Happify.com, accessed June 3, 2024, https://www.happify.com/hd/the-science-behind-gratitude/#:~:text=Research%20by%20UC%20Davis%20psychologist,well%E2%80%91being%20and%20life%20satisfaction.

Focusing on the things for which we are grateful can help shift our perspective from negative to positive, leading to increased feelings of happiness, joy, and contentment. Expressing gratitude to others can strengthen relationships and increase feelings of connection and empathy. Gratitude boosts resilience. Gratitude helps us cope with challenging situations. It focuses us on the positive aspects of our lives, even during difficult times.

Gratitude isn't just for special occasions. Yes, you might express gratitude after receiving a raise, but you can also be thankful for something as simple as having the door held open for you. Even these small moments of gratitude are beneficial: "Research by UC Davis psychologist Robert Emmons, author of *Thanks!: How the New Science of Gratitude Can Make You Happier*, shows that simply keeping a gratitude journal and regularly reflecting, in writing, on moments for which we are thankful can significantly increase well-being and life satisfaction."[35]

Every day, when you first wake up, you might take a moment and say grace over that for which you are thankful. Cultivate this reflection as a daily habit. See the impact that these ten seconds may have upon you over time.

---

35   Carpenter, "The Science behind Gratitude (and How It Can Change Your Life)."

REFLECTION ON GRATITUDE

Let's pause, intentionally, for a moment and think of four people in your life for whom you want to express gratitude:

Think about the first person that comes to your mind for whom you want to express gratitude. Imagine them before you. What is the color of their eyes? Go back to the first memory you have of this person. Where did you meet? What time of year? What time of day? How were you feeling? Send silent gratitude to this person.

Think of a second person who means a lot to you. Imagine that this person is very happy. Send silent gratitude.

Think of yourself when you were eight years old. What did you look like? What were you wearing? Send silent gratitude to your eight-year-old self.

Think of someone you love who has passed away. Give that person a hug. Send silent gratitude to that loved one.

Practice Generosity

The University of Notre Dame's Science of Generosity Project defines generosity as "giving good things to others freely and abundantly."[36] Practicing generosity is a fundamental component of all religions and spiritual practices of humans.

Practicing generosity means cultivating a genuine concern for the well-being of others and a deep connection to humanity. It means adopting an attitude of selflessness and compassion in one's actions

---

36 Christian Smith, "What Makes Us Generous?," Science of Generosity, University of Notre Dame, May 27, 2014, https://generosityresearch.nd.edu/news/what-makes-us-generous/#:~:text=By%20%E2%80%9Cgenerosity%2C%E2%80%9D%20I%20mean,actual%20practice%20of%20giving%20liberally.

and interactions with others. A philanthropist will develop a compassionate heart and extend kindness and support to others without expecting anything in return.

Practicing generosity also means orienting yourself to an abundance mindset rather than a scarcity mindset.[37] There is enough to share. This giving does not diminish one's own well-being or resources. Generosity fosters gratitude, contentment, and a sense of abundance, counteracting feelings of greed, attachment, or fear of scarcity.

I'd like you to consider a meditation in generosity. Find a quiet place. Pay attention to your breathing. You can close your eyes. As you relax, think of two thoughts.

• **Thought One**: Think of a time someone was generous to you. How did you feel? Retrace your life. Has someone stopped to help you when your car had a flat tire or was broken down on the side of the road? Did someone take time to teach you a skill or a sport? When you lost a loved one, who was there comforting you? Reflect on as many of these moments as possible. Think about those people who have helped you and who have done so without asking for anything in return.

• **Thought Two**: Now, switch gears. Think about a time when you were generous to someone else. The size or the scope doesn't matter. You have a lifetime to consider. Think over the course of your years. Think of each instance when you were generous to someone else without any thought of return.

37 "Cultivating Abundance: A Shift from Scarcity to Abundance Mindset in Charitable Giving," The Physician Philanthropist, November 15, 2023, https://www.thephysician-philanthropist.com/blog/cultivating-abundance-a-shift-from-scarcity-to-abundance-mindset-in-charitable-giving.

After you complete this visualization, write down what you discover. Make two lists—one that reflects the moments of your life when someone showed you generosity and one where you in turn were generous. Revisit these generosity lists from time to time. Add to your lists as memories return to you or when generosity occurs in the future—both from others and from yourself.

When you complete this meditation on generosity, how do you feel?

This exercise is designed to trigger the feeling of the "Helper's High," a concept that "arose in the 1980s and has been confirmed in various studies since then. The Helper's High consists of positive emotions that may arise following selfless service to others. Greater health and increased longevity are associated with this psychological state."[38] At the National Institutes of Health, neuroscientist Jorge Moll found that when individuals donate money, the mesolimbic system in the brain is activated. This system reinforces stimuli such as sex, food, drugs, and money by releasing feel-good neurotransmitters such as oxytocin and vasopressin. Consequently, when people express generosity to others, such as volunteering or donating money, they feel good and are more likely to repeat these behaviors. Confirming these correlations, other studies have revealed that the thought of helping others activates the same part of the brain as thinking about receiving rewards or experiencing pleasure.

Read

Reading provides you the opportunity to step into the mind of another person. When you engage in reading, you suspend the stream

---

38   Larry Dossey, "The Helper's High," ScienceDirect, 2018, https://www.sciencedirect. com/science/article/abs/pii/S1550830718304178?via%3Dihub.

of thoughts in your brain and replace them with the voice of another. Read books and materials that fall outside your normal interests.

Reading is a form of travel. It lets you escape your physical boundaries and gives you a moment outside yourself.

While examining the individualistic voices of authors, Russian literary theorist Mikhail Bakhtin proposed that literature exists in a continuum of human dialogue.[39] There is no separation of the speaker and the words spoken. As we dive into a novel, we immerse ourselves in the voice of the author, and if the author is exceptionally talented, we find ourselves in a heterogenous mix of voices in a carnival-like world of speech. For the philanthropist, reading is an opportunity to quiet our own voice and, in doing so, expand our empathy through the assumption of the thoughts of another.

Travel

Understanding comes through experience. Imagination is a powerful tool, but experience is essential, and travel is about having new experiences. Travel forces us to escape the insulation of our comfort zones and face new situations, strengthening our ability to empathize with a broader range of people. When you agree to open yourself up to new experiences and make the decision to travel, you are actively pursuing the understanding of different cultures, peoples, and places. When traveling, a heightened sense of observation and otherness allows new experiences and impressions to flow into your consciousness more freely.

As author David Mura writes in his 2018 book *A Stranger's Journey: Race, Identity, and Narrative Craft in Writing*, "We are not all-knowing creatures. If we live in a village … we think our truth

---

39 Mikhail Bakhtin, *The Dialogic Imagination*, trans. Caryl Emerson and Michael Holquist, University of Texas Press, Austin (1981).

is the only truth; we think the way we see ourselves is the only way to see ourselves. But if a stranger walks into our village, or if we … walk into a village of strangers, we are suddenly aware that there are other ways of looking at the world; there are other ways of looking at ourselves, at who we are, at our place in the world, at the ways we identify ourselves."

The founding father of Rotary, Paul Harris, knew the importance of travel. When we travel, we learn that there are hundreds of ways to live on this planet. There are hundreds of ways to raise our children, hundreds of ways to reside, whether in homes, apartments, or tree houses. Hundreds of ways to worship, eat, and work. And perhaps the most important realization is that our way of life is not necessarily the only way.

Practice Listening

When you listen to others and then reflect back to them your best understanding of what they said, you build an emotional bond with them. When you feel that someone is really listening to you, attempting to understand not only what you are saying but also the feelings behind the words you are using to convey them, you can't help but feel kindly toward them. This attachment reinforces trust. When you listen, for a moment you can quiet the voice in your head and open yourself to experience the other person's point of view. To do so, you must actively stop yourself from thinking of your next comment or response. You must pause that mental activity and be a quiet receiver. Try to be more aware of this practice as you listen to others.

Make Everything You Do Important

When all else fails, go out and make everything you do count. Make everything you do important.

If you are stuck in the development of your philanthropic plan, reset your mindset. You are a hero, walking this earth on your journey. Consider that all things in your path are important. Every interaction is a chance to lift someone's spirits or to make a difference. Engage your life with this purpose, and meaning will emerge. Visualize your hero story. Every interaction is a moment where you can accomplish your mission.

Play a game—with everyone you meet, believe they have information that might help you with your mission of the day and, likewise, that you have information that may help them. Play the game long enough, and you'll start to realize that it may not be a game.

Remember the credo of George Washington that we mentioned in part 1: "Never let an indigent person ask without receiving something if you have the means." Live by that thought—or at least by a contemporary analogue—never turn away empty handed a person in need. If someone asks you for help, and they are in need, be there to help. You may not give them exactly that for which they are asking, but give them what you can by the means you have, whether financial, physical, or thoughtful.

Establish Boundaries

It's also OK to establish boundaries as a philanthropist. The cultivation of empathy can result in the world overwhelming you from time to time. As you work to see outside yourself and take on the viewpoints of others, you can be overcome with their emotions. As you lower your barriers to sense others' feelings, you need to also be aware of the times to raise your guard.

How often have you been watching television or surfing the internet when, unexpectedly, a commercial for a nonprofit comes on, graphically depicting starving children or abused animals and then asking for a contribution. This attempt at fundraising is more aptly described as philanthropic pornography. It's OK to turn away from this intrusion of images. These commercials cross an emotional boundary and are often exploitative. I mention it to illustrate that not everyone who approaches your philanthropic side will do so with the best of intentions or the most ethical of means. Not to diminish the causes that these commercials purport to present, but in this world, where we are intentionally cultivating empathy as a virtue of the philanthropic way, we must equally protect the philanthropist and advise that it is not only socially acceptable but also fundamental to your well-being to protect your mental health through the establishment of emotional boundaries.

How Does the Power of Empathy Support You in Your Philanthropic Way?

In part 1, we realized that a key role of the philanthropist in society is to restrict asset bases for the use of nonprofit organizations to address gaps, injustices, and disparities that arise in democratic capitalism. As you get started, it's hard to know how you, individually, will *be* as a philanthropist—what missions to pursue, what assets to donate, or to which nonprofits. Empathy is the spark that will light the philanthropic fire in you. Here are a few thoughts on the power of empathy to support your philanthropic way:

- Empathy is a frame of mind where you set ego aside for a moment. When you do so, you become receptive to causes that are meaningful to you.

- Whether you are a director entering a board meeting, a C-suite executive of a nonprofit, an employee, volunteer, or donor, empathy is a critical skill for you to cultivate in service of mission. It enables you to engage in disagreements in a civil and professional manner. It allows you to be open to points of view that may challenge your perspective. Should a board make a decision with which you might disagree, empathy allows you to be humble, defer to the group, and thereafter speak with one shared voice with your colleagues. It allows you to realize that everyone comes to the table with different knowledge and experiences that inform their perspective. The power of the collective is captured when everyone's voice is respected, notwithstanding any disagreement.

- Empathy enables you to evaluate the individuals who lead any nonprofit organization you might support. As you review part 3, you will see how you may use empathy to understand the rapport and relationship between the CEO and board chair of a nonprofit organization to anticipate the organization's trajectory. This will give you subtle cues to the potential of the organization or, alternatively, its problems.

- In part 4, you will work on the creation and drafting of your philanthropic plan. You will see that your expression of philanthropy, including the recipient of your generosity and any restrictions associated with your charitable giving, will reflect your empathic self.

In the places of this world that call to you, that compel your heart to love in such a fierce way that you can heal anything, this is where we understand what it is to be human. Empathy for others can help you realize how fortunate you are, and sometimes, when you are giving from the heart, it will bring you joy and happiness, lighting the moments of darkness. This is philanthropic empathy. It is an intentional focus on *philos anthropos*. When you live like this, you realize that philanthropic empathy carries an acceptance of all points of view. Not that all points of view are correct, but that every one of us has a right to a point of view. We're not being philanthropic if we don't attempt to listen to all voices, even if we disagree with some, or all, of them. It is philanthropic empathy that causes the Rotarians to ask of every interaction whether it is *fair* and *beneficial "to all concerned."* Philanthropic empathy will lead you to an inclusion of all perspectives as you evaluate this world.

CHAPTER 6

The Ethics of Information and Truth

An interesting by-product of an increased sense of empathy is a desire to get to the truth of all matters. There's a reason the first question of the Rotarian Four-Way Test asks, "Is it the *truth*?" You might view the pursuit of empathy as a desire to gain new information to drive insights. There's a certain honesty that empathic living necessitates. You should be open to correction and allow your thinking to evolve as you gain new information and experience. To be a successful philanthropist, you need to live pursuant to certain ethics of information and truth. The search for truth is a difficult and personal concept that will require you to overcome information relativism and deeply imbedded biases.

What do I mean by the ethics of information and truth?

This discipline arises from a moral obligation of the philanthropist to seek out as much information as possible in pursuit of wisdom in our world. While there's no such thing as an absolute truth, as your philanthropic empathy increases, you should feel a pull to learn more, in as honest a manner as possible, about the world and people around you. The motto of Phi Beta Kappa, the nonprofit academic organization founded by five students at William & Mary in 1776 during the American Revolution, applies to all philanthropists: "A Love of Learning is the Guide to Life."

We live in an unprecedented time of recorded knowledge, language, content, and information. Gordon Moore's observation in 1965 remains true—that the number of transistors in a dense integrated circuit, such as in a computer, which doubles every year, correlates to a similar expansion of speed, data storage, and advanced computing power. This doubling also has a direct relation to the exponential growth in knowledge and content we are witnessing. And yet, we don't know what to do with this information. We don't understand the legal implications of such information, the effect such information has on the economy, on rational decision-making, not to mention the power to use data to manipulate minds and deceive peoples. The emergence of "big data" is a modern-day example of a technological leap for which we are unprepared to understand the ethical implications.

With any decision you make, there is, in the present time, an unlimited amount of data and information that you, as a human, might consider. Such volume and breadth of data, big and small, can cause you to fall into informational relativism, where there are no truths or where the exception might be given undue weight, influence, or importance. Probabilities of outcome are no longer considered. The origin of such informational manipulation is often biases of the ego, for which the individual isn't adequately self-aware.

TYPES OF BIAS

Here are just a few of the biases to which most of us are prone:

• **Confirmation bias**: A person seeks out information that supports their existing beliefs while ignoring or dismissing information that contradicts those beliefs. This can lead to poor decision-making, as the person may miss important information that could change their opinion.

• **Stereotyping**: A person makes assumptions about an individual or group based on a stereotype, without considering their unique qualities or circumstances, such as assuming all teenagers are lazy.

• **Groupthink**: Members of a group make a decision based on the desire for harmony or conformity within the group rather than considering all available options and perspectives. This can lead to poor consideration of dissenting opinions.

• **Dunning-Kruger effect**: A person with little expertise or ability assumes they have superior expertise or ability. This overestimation occurs because they don't have enough knowledge to know that they don't have enough knowledge.

• **Availability bias**: A person makes a decision based on the information that is most readily available to them rather than considering all available information. For example, a person may be more likely to be afraid of flying after a recent plane crash, even though flying is statistically safer than driving.

• **Halo effect**: A person makes a positive or negative judgment about an individual based on one positive or negative trait without considering other aspects of their personality or behavior, such as assuming that someone who is attractive must also be intelligent and kind.

- **Sunk cost fallacy**: A person continues to invest time, money, or effort into a project or endeavor, even though it's no longer viable or profitable, because they have already invested so much.

- **Racial and tribal biases**: The worst of the biases are racial and tribal biases, which are forms of prejudice and discrimination based on a person's perceived racial or tribal identity.

Racial bias refers to preconceived notions, stereotypes, and discriminatory attitudes or behaviors directed toward individuals or groups based on their race or ethnicity. Race is a social construct, and there is no scientific basis for categorizing people into distinct racial groups. However, racial bias can lead to discriminatory actions, unequal treatment, and systemic racism, perpetuating social and economic disparities among groups with different physical features.

Tribal bias, sometimes referred to as ethnocentrism or xenophobia, is a form of prejudice based on a person's ethnic, religious, business, or political affiliation. Tribalism often involves a strong sense of loyalty and identity to one's own tribe while harboring negative attitudes toward other tribes. This bias can lead to conflicts, discrimination, and a lack of cooperation in communities, hampering societal cohesion and advancement.

Biases can be so imbedded in the human experience and psyche that it's hard to shake them. These biases can also result in the creation of systems and structures in society to advance one group over another. Sometimes folks aren't always left behind by a technological leap. More often groups are *kept* behind.

These biases have existed throughout human history and continue to drive societal issues. Biases are ingrained in our individual psyches and manifest in various ways, influencing attitudes, behaviors, and social structures. Unfortunately, the foregoing list is nonexhaustive.

All biases share the common result of poor decision-making, which leads to inefficiencies and injustices. In the nonprofit boardroom or workspaces, you can see how these biases can be detrimental to an organization. Yet how do we actively train ourselves to be self-aware and mindful of these distortions?

We find ourselves in a world where society doesn't fully understand the ethical implications of data, big and small, whether in healthcare, consumer protection, insurance actuarial projections, or any number of fields. To develop a philanthropic plan, we each have the responsibility to be aware of the need for a personal ethic of information, a pursuit of neutral, objective analysis, to understand and see the perspective of others. This is the key to success in the boardroom, the workplace, or a philanthropic plan.

Biases in the Structuring of Data into Information

Data, in and of itself, should be without bias, yet it's the structuring and organization of data into information where a person's point of view may influence the presentation or projected meaning. Being empathic with the viewpoint of the person who structured the data into information will make a difference in the decisions you make.

I can give you an example.

The GDP is a monetary measure of the market value of all the final goods and services produced and sold in a specific time period by a country. Many people consider GDP to be the "world's most powerful statistical indicator of national development and progress."[40] We even used GDP in part 1 of this handbook to compare against growth rates in revenue and wealth of nonprofit organizations.

If the GDP for a nation were to go negative for two calendar quarters, we might say that nation is in recession. In the United States, our Federal Reserve closely examines GDP to understand our country's economic performance and, as necessary, raises or lowers interest rates. GDP is a central tool for policymakers when making decisions that depend on an assessment of growth or contraction of an economy. Yet how valuable and accurate is GDP for purposes of such grand macroeconomic decisions that affect all of us?

While the economist Simon Kuznets is credited with the invention of the GDP in 1932 as an attempt to estimate the national income of the United States to understand the full extent of the Great Depression, it was John Maynard Keynes who developed the modern definition of GDP during World War II. In 1940, Keynes, while working in the UK Treasury, published an essay complaining about the inadequacy of economic statistics to calculate what Britain could produce with its available resources. He argued that the paucity of such data made it difficult to estimate Britain's capacity for mobilization and war.

According to Keynes, the estimate of national income should be the sum of private consumption, investment, and government spending. Wartime necessities, with a focus on governmental spending, drove his method of calculating GDP, and it soon found acceptance

---

40 Philipp Lepenies, *The Power of a Single Number: A Political History of GDP (New York: Columbia University, 2016)*.

around the world even after the war was over. The Keynesian approach to economics continues to this day.[41]

One can see, though, that GDP as a metric doesn't include significant areas of internal value in an economy. Some argue that GDP is a poor indicator of the welfare of a society. GDP leaves out meaningful areas of production, such as the nontransactional goods and services like domestic work necessary to maintain a household. It fails to account for the costs imposed on human health and the environment as a by-product of the production or consumption of a country's output.

In our area of interest, GDP additionally fails to account for charitable giving to and expenditures from nonprofit organizations. Indeed, this handbook holds that the well-being of a society or country is based upon the amount of assets that philanthropists restrict to permanent endowments in nonprofits. GDP as a metric contains no information from the nonprofit sector regarding its endowed and restricted assets bases, with their vast, diversified investments in governmental bonds and publicly traded companies. Policymakers and economists often treat GDP as an all-encompassing unit to signify a country's development, combining its economic prosperity and societal well-being, but that isn't the full picture.

GDP is divorced from metrics of charitable giving. If you use GDP with that perspective in mind, it might be a foil to economic trendlines in philanthropy, as we used it in some of the graphics and examples in part 1 of this handbook. Knowing what is not included in GDP allows us to use that metric in more novel ways, including a variety of comparisons against purely charitable metrics. We can

---

41 Amit Kapoor and Bibek Debroy, "GDP Is not a Measure of Human Well-Being," *Harvard Business Review, October 4, 2019,* https://hbr.org/2019/10/gdp-is-not-a-measure-of-human-well-being.

examine fluctuations over time in the amount of charitable contributions reported on all US tax returns against changes in the United States GDP over the same period. Those types of comparisons may be used to test theories of causality. Do changes in size of the nonprofit sector from year to year have any effect on GDP over time? This is a key point of the ethics of information and truth. Understand the structure and organization of the information with which you are working. That will help you to understand how you may use such information. Without that discipline, your decision-making may slip into biases and unintended points of view.

The importance of the philanthropist to achieve a certain level of neutrality to the world, without bias, coupled with a desire to understand more and more of the world around us, cannot be stressed enough. Without a moral obligation to seek out as much information as possible in pursuit of deeper understanding and correction of prior mistakes, you won't be able to evaluate effectively the performance of nonprofits or the impact of your philanthropic investments. You will not have the foresight to be effective. The ethics of information and truth should drive you to set boundaries on your empathy. Such ethics will enable you to rank, differentiate, and prioritize nonprofit organizations and causes. Absent the ethics of information and truth, you will not be equipped to evaluate, assess, and compare nonprofit organizations as beneficiaries of your philanthropic plan.

Beware the Power of Philanthropy

If you're amplifying your empathic abilities through the pursuit of greater amounts of unbiased information in search of insights and truths, you must take time to reflect on the power of philanthropy in society.

In most democratic capitalist societies, the power of philanthropy is concentrated in a few individuals and families.

In 2013, the IRS began to require separate reporting for estates of $50 million or more in tax returns. In every year from 2013 to 2017, an average of 186 decedents per year reported wealth of this size. This small group also gave the majority of all charitable dollars reported on all estate tax returns in the United States, a country with a population of over 300 million.

It's always been this way in the United States. In 1916–21, over 30 percent of all charitable estate dollars came from thirty-five decedents. In 1922, over 55 percent of all charitable estate dollars came from sixteen decedents.

There are several ways to think about this type of information:

At least the wealthy are doing their part in a manner that aligns with their ability to contribute.

In a capitalist society, this is a basic tenet of philanthropy—charities compete for wealth to achieve positive impact in communities. This is just another type of competition in a capitalist market.

Still, this is a lot of power in the hands of a few, wielding its effect upon the many. What distortions might arise?

Also, just because a few can make such an economic impact, that doesn't change or affect any human with a desire to be a philanthropist. The way of philanthropy may and should be pursued by all as a virtue for all, providing personal meaning to life.

If the singular motive for profit, absent any other constraints, can lead to economic disparities, gaps, and injustices in society, then how should we pursue our own wealth accumulation and then wield the power of that wealth through philanthropy? This is sometimes called the "philanthropic paradox." As the authors of the *Impact Investing Handbook* explain, philanthropy often aims "to solve problems that may have been caused by the source of the donor's wealth." Andrew Carnegie may be known as one of the greatest philanthropists of the modern era, but you have to also consider the exploitation of labor in the steel industry that generated his wealth. John D. Rockefeller may be known for the many causes and institutions he supported, but consider the profound negative effects to the climate that come directly from Rockefeller's accumulation of oil wealth.[42]

For those of you at that inflection point where you turn the corner from wealth accumulation to philanthropy, it's a strange moment of change. It's a time to consider your own philanthropic paradox. What has been your lifetime impact upon humanity's collective resources?

Perhaps these questions don't matter. What matters in the end is that, if you don't pay close attention and respect the power of philanthropy, it can increase your ego while diminishing your empathy. It can create biases in your decision-making. Beware the power within philanthropy. Condition it with humility and self-awareness. Recognize that you are one human in a history of billions who, one day, will be dead and gone.

---

42   Steven Godeke and Patrick Briaud, *Impact Investing Handbook: An Implementation Guide for Practitioners*, Rockefeller Philanthropy Advisors, accessed March 7, 2024, https://www.rockpa.org/wp-content/uploads/2020/10/RPA-Impact-Investing-Handbook-1.pdf.

CHAPTER 7

The Discipline of Foresight

The capacity for language is inherent to humans. It sets us apart from all other animals on Earth. Not just the capacity for speech but the ability to create a series of symbols that reflect the sounds of speech and may be recorded in a two-dimensional manner, such as in books or electronic files. The emergence of language enabled us to measure the world. As our ancestors recorded events, they became aware of the peculiar sequence of time. Time might first have been measured in the count of days. With each recording of the day, our ancestors began to document recurring details, such as the position of the stars in the sky and the changing of seasons and weather patterns. Memories in the form of written word, represented through language and dated in relation to days and years past, began the foundation of knowledge and the sense that humans move through time in one direction, flowing from the present to the future, leaving behind the past like the wake of a boat on the water.

A curious thing about this notion of time—the knowledge of time makes people think they can predict the future and anticipate events to come. The evolutionary emergence of advanced "symbolizing" capacity enabled humans to transcend the dictates of our immediate environment and made us unique in our power to shape our life circumstances. With forethought, people are contributors to their lives and not just products of them. Regardless of whether you think of time as an illusion, to a farmer the measure of time identifies the optimal time to plant. In the jungle and wild plains, the primordial human's ability to forecast the imminent future was the difference that turned humans from prey into the apex predator. Just as language begat the concept of time, so too emerged the idea of foresight—thinking beforehand, planning before action, premeditation.

It's no wonder that Prometheus is also known as the Titan of foresight. Indeed, the very name *Prometheus* translates from the ancient Greek word meaning "foresight." In the ancient worldview, we see the emergence of the word *philanthropy* from the archetypal deity of foresight, who created humankind. That is a powerful historical connection that should not be lost on the philanthropist.

Foresight draws upon self-awareness and the pursuit of hidden insights and meaning in the world, outside ego and biases. It's not that the philanthropist is unable to act in self-interest, but it's important for the philanthropist to be honest and aware of their own emotions, with a goal to understand the underlying factors that gave rise to such feelings. When the philanthropist achieves this level of empathic self-awareness, foresight will manifest, and your philanthropic plan will begin to emerge.

FORESIGHT EXERCISE

Pause for a moment. Consider your surroundings. Look around you. Are you outside, amid buildings, roads, and automobiles? Maybe you're inside, sitting in a chair. Have you considered who made the chair, who brought it here to your location? What are the materials made of? There's a screw that interlocks with a bolt to hold two pieces together. How did that screw come to be in this chair, from what factory? What machine was used to fabricate the screw? What were the mathematics to calculate the spiral and interlock with the bolt? Who identified the mathematics, when, and in what sequence of concepts? Think back further: What metallurgical sciences were employed to create the compound that made the screw? And think about all the people, all the way back to the accomplishments of the Industrial Age and to the metal arts of the Bronze Age, all these factors and people coming together to create this basic screw to hold together your chair, where you sit and read a page like this, at this moment. If you think back further and further to trace the connections of knowledge, science, and art that brought you to this chair today, held together by such a screw, you will eventually get to the historical point of the emergence of written language and, before that, language itself.

You live in the present world of creations, all around you, everywhere you look—creations that are the product of generations of foresight going back hundreds of years, if not millennia. The screw that holds together your chair is the product of foresight of millions of individuals who came before. If you're going to be a philanthropist, you must never lose sight of the role that you play in this continuum of human experience, where the present rests on the shoulders of our forebears and the future present lies in your imagination.

If you consider that our species emerged into being three hundred thousand years ago, and if we live as long as the typical mammalian species, we will last about two million years. If the human race were a single individual, she would be about ten years old now. But humans are not typical. If we are careful, why would we die off in two million years? We might exist for as long as Earth remains habitable. If we dream, however, to take to the skies and achieve interplanetary travel and colonization of the universe, then we could exist for billions of years more.

The last two centuries brought massive technological achievements, but they also brought the risk of global nuclear destruction, the potential for extreme climate change, and the possibility that artificial intelligence might overtake humankind. As time goes on, this pattern of technological advancement coupled with greater and greater existential risks will continue to follow us. It's through an investment in foresight that the philanthropist works to address such risks. It's only through foresight that our technology, emerging from our centuries of progress, science, and knowledge, institutionalized and endowed in our species from one person to the next, one generation to the subsequent, will work in cooperation and in sync with our natural world.

It is a profound exercise of foresight to become aware through scientific inquiry that the universe is 13.8 billion years old. Our planet, Earth, which gave rise to our human consciousness, was born 4.5 billion years ago. In this vast expanse of space, this mote of dust in a sunbeam was able to experience consciousness. Any number of events can wipe out the planet Earth or its inhabitants, including the inevitable expansion of the sun to absorb Earth and all life contained hereon. A vision of a future humankind that has taken to the stars and become a multiplanetary species reflects many aspirations of the philanthropic way. Such undertakings exist in the hearts of true philanthropists. As we look up to the stars from this small planet, we can dream of a future of adventure, exploration, and ever-expanding knowledge.

CHAPTER 8

How Does the Way of Philanthropy Assist You in Your Role as Philanthropist?

Philanthropy is a virtue of humankind that is key to our survival. It is a feature in democratic capitalist societies that balances corporations' striving for profit with an urge for our community to come together through mutually agreed-upon ethics and moral behavior. As technology disrupts our economy, philanthropy reaches for appropriate ethical responses. Empathy helps you hear your calling and find the causes to which your attention is drawn. Empathy makes you aware of gaps, disparities, and injustices in society. Empathy inspires you toward an ethic of information and truth.

An ethic of information and truth gives you the insights, tools, and metrics to assess both (1) the issues you wish to confront and (2) the organizations in the landscape that might be best suited to address such issues. If an ethic of information and truth is turned inward to examine self, it is a source of humility. This mindset, this steady pursuit of insights, enables you to consider the balance of your physical impacts on this world during your lifetime against your philanthropic impacts that may continue after your death.

It's foresight, drawing from empathy and an ethically driven pursuit of information and truth, that opens you to consider novel solutions and, in doing so, helps you to identify like-minded nonprofit organizations to support. If the honest, fact-finding cultivation of empathy attracts your philanthropic calling, foresight focuses your thinking on specific nonprofit organizations to endow as beneficiaries of your philanthropic plan. Foresight is a means through which we may help human society to meet the challenges of emerging technology while avoiding setbacks for the endowing of humanity.

As you consider the world around you, these three disciplines of philanthropy can ground you. They can help you to be mindful of your place in the continuum of history. These disciplines can remind you of the many gifts endowed in your life from the generations who came before. You can apply these disciplines to your awareness and understanding of the challenges we expect to emerge in our current age of information, including the rise of artificial intelligence, deepfakes that bend reality and truth, and misinformation corrupting our endowment of knowledge. Today's disruptive technologies require, now more than ever, that the philanthropist be well focused in these three disciplines.

For those nonprofit organizations to which you're attracted, you'll be better equipped to examine their leadership, prioritize their needs, and assess their abilities. Whether you're a donor to a public charity, a director on a board, a CEO, or a volunteer, these three disciplines are required of you each day in this job. Whether you're entering the boardroom or volunteering in a programmatic setting, this is the mindset you should bring. This is the expectation of performance when you engage in philanthropy. This is also the meaning of philanthropy in the ancient world, as might have been discussed at Plato's Academy. This is the level of mindfulness expected of the philanthropist.

To conclude this part 2, I want to share with you a quote from Paul Harris, published in *The Rotarian* in 1945 at the end of World War II, which I think equally applies to the role of the philanthropist at the dawn of the age of information, notwithstanding how different our time is today:

> I would like to think that the pioneering days of Rotary have only just begun. There are just as many new things to be done as ever there were. Kaleidoscopic changes are taking place, many of them without our will. Even to hang on to the fringe of this fast-changing world is about all most of us can do. Rotary simply must continue to pioneer or be left in the rear of progress.[43]

---

43   Paul Harris in *The Rotarian, February 1945.*

PART 3

The Aspirational Nonprofit

*The great use of a life is to spend it
for something that outlasts it.*

—WILLIAM JAMES

CHAPTER 9

Designing the Contemporary Nonprofit Organization

I f you're not from Cleveland, or even Ohio, I wouldn't expect the name Frederick Harris Goff to ring any bells. And yet his creativity and thoughtfulness revolutionized philanthropy for the twentieth century. He is the originator of the modern-day community foundation.

Fred was born on December 15, 1858, in Blackbury, Illinois, just a few years before the American Civil War. In his early years, his family moved around looking for work. In 1863, Fred came to Cleveland in a boxcar with his older brother, riding along with their family horse, to meet his parents, who'd gone ahead. He was no more than five or six years old.[44] Fred was not born to wealth. From reading about him, I get the sense that his parents raised him to be independent and highly focused on right and wrong. I imagine the Goff family as straightforward, working-class people.

---

44 "Frederick H. Goff: National Intellectual Treasure," Cleveland Foundation, accessed March 18, 2024, https://www.clevelandfoundation100.org/foundation-of-change/invention/frederick-goff/.

Fred swept floors and took whatever jobs he could find to attend the University of Michigan, where he graduated in 1881 with a bachelor's degree in philosophy. Later, he worked as a librarian to make his way through law school. In 1883, he was admitted to the Ohio bar and started a solo practice in Cleveland.

Quickly, he merged with other groups of lawyers, eventually landing in the firm that would become Jones Day. Through these mergers, he was able to focus his practice as a corporate attorney, working on business reorganizations, antitrust issues, and complicated financing arrangements. Fred was smart. Early in his career as an attorney, he caught the eye of John D. Rockefeller, who had started Standard Oil Company in Cleveland. Fred's firm served as Rockefeller's outside counsel, and I understand Rockefeller asked Fred on more than one occasion to work directly for him in his company.

By all accounts, Fred seemed to have been liked by everyone with whom he came into contact. He famously helped mediate a war between two Cleveland streetcar companies—one public, one private. The townspeople of Glenville, a small town outside Cleveland where he lived, actually protested at Fred's house one night because they wanted him to be mayor. He wasn't interested. Eventually, possibly as a consequence of too many late-night protests, Fred acquiesced and was elected mayor. In his time as mayor, he helped get rid of racetrack gambling in the town and eventually guided Glenville to be annexed into Cleveland.[45]

Fred was a family man, devoted to his wife, Frances, whom he wed in 1894. They had three children together. Frances shared her husband's belief in planning for the future, both in personal and civic

---

45   John Kroll, "Frederick Goff's Legacy Lives On within the Cleveland Foundation: PD 175," *Cleveland Plain Dealer, November 23, 2017,* https://www.cleveland.com/business/2017/11/frederick_goffs_legacy_lives_o.html.

affairs. Frances was a graduate of Vassar College and was active in their alumnae affairs, among many other charitable pursuits. Their relationship seems to reflect a true partnership. Fred shared the creation of the first community foundation with Frances, valuing her input and recommendations. According to a local historical society, Frances "toiled unceasingly with her husband in the foundation and could genuinely be called a cofounder."[46]

In 1908, Fred left the practice of law to start a new chapter in his life as the president of the Cleveland Trust, a small Ohio bank. In doing so, he took a significant pay cut. But he wanted to pursue the opportunity because he knew the impact he could make on Cleveland in this role. Under his leadership, the bank's offices increased from "15 to 52, its depositors from 70,000 to 397,000, and its resources from $30 million to $176 million by 1923."[47] The Cleveland Foundation notes that Fred "encouraged Cleveland Trust to offer reasonable mortgage terms, easing the path to home ownership for the working classes, especially those of African-American descent."[48] His sense of ethics ingrained in him by his parents from childhood made Fred a man who had empathy for others and approached his community from an egalitarian perspective. He showed fairness to all. His drive for learning and the betterment of his community gave him the foresight to seek long-term solutions for the problems around him.

In addition to standard banking services, the bank administered the bequests of many large estates held in trust funds. That work reminded Fred how often provisions for the charitable use of income became obsolete or counterproductive over time. He had seen this as

46   "Frederick Goff," Bratenahl Historical Society, accessed March 18, 2024, https://bratenahlhistorical.org/index.php/frederick-goff/.

47   "Goff, Frederick H.," Encyclopedia of Cleveland History, Case Western Reserve University, accessed March 18, 2024, https://case.edu/ech/articles/g/goff-frederick-h.

48   "Frederick H. Goff: National Intellectual Treasure."

an attorney. Now he was seeing it as a banker: "He began to dream of breaking the stranglehold that bequests that had outlived their designated charitable purposes exerted on vast amounts of capital. At a time when social needs were great, it troubled him that so much wealth was uselessly held in the icy grip of irrevocable wills."[49] Fred called this phenomenon the "dead hand." It would reach from the grave to exert control over charitable assets, without any awareness of the then-current issues of the day. In his early years at the bank, he began to wonder how to release the grip of the invisible dead hand.

Fred once wrote, "How fine it would be" if an individual who was "about to make a will could go to a permanently established organization … and say, 'Here is a large sum of money. I want to leave it to be used for the good of the community, but I have no way of knowing what will be the greatest need 50 years from now. Therefore, I place it in your hands to determine what should be done.'"[50]

Ultimately, Fred had an idea: What if one entity, like a community trust or foundation, could manage multiple charitable trusts that might be invested together as a general pool? He took great interest in the creation of the Rockefeller Foundation in 1913 as well as many other private foundations and public charities of the era. His thinking was also impacted by Leonard Porter Ayres's book *Seven Great Foundations*, which proposed that "great" foundations are large scale and secular, have broad geographic purpose, and have exceptional boards drawn to the foundation for altruistic purposes.[51] Fred spent time consider-

---

49   "Frederick H. Goff: National Intellectual Treasure."

50   "An Idea Whose Time Had Come," Cleveland Foundation, accessed March 18, 2024, https://www.clevelandfoundation100.org/foundation-of-change/invention/introduction/.

51   Leonard P. Ayres, *Seven Great Foundations* (New York: Russell Sage Foundation, 1911), pp. 11–12. Available on the internet as part of the Philanthropy Classics Access Project at www.hks.harvard.edu/hauser/philanthropyclassics/pdf_files/ayres.pdf.

ing the importance of an independent board of civic leaders. Who would compose the board? How would they govern? The Cleveland Foundation, the first-ever "community foundation," was the product of his careful study of these foundations.

Fred looked to draw primarily from the private foundation model, but with some important distinctions. In particular, the Cleveland Foundation was to be public rather than private, with a goal of giving ordinary citizens, not just the ultrawealthy, the opportunity to contribute to a local fund that addressed local issues just as large foundations like the Rockefeller Foundation did. His vision was to pool Cleveland's charitable resources into a single, permanent endowment for the city's advancement. Community leaders would then forever distribute the interest therefrom to fund "such charitable purposes as will best make for the mental, moral, and physical improvement of the inhabitants of Cleveland."[52]

Fred convinced the bank board to adopt a resolution and declaration of trust to establish the Cleveland Foundation on January 2, 1914. He designed it to be nonsectarian and focused geographically to serve only Cleveland. He built in a provision that funds established in the foundation could be modified as local conditions changed. As a *community* foundation, the Cleveland Foundation had a board made up of prominent local citizens who would serve for limited terms without pay. This board was accountable to the community and operated transparently.

Within six weeks of opening the Cleveland Foundation, Fred announced that the first act of the foundation would be to undertake "a great social and economic survey of Cleveland, to uncover the causes

---

52 "Frederick Goff," Bratenahl Historical Society.

of poverty and crime and point out the cure."[53] The survey would be a way for the foundation to increase public awareness of the problems facing Cleveland during that period of rapid urbanization. At the time, Cleveland was the fifth-largest city in the United States, with a major port on the Great Lakes and a concentration of businesses in the steel industry. The foundation's survey was also to be the blueprint to guide future grant making after the endowment was established.

In response, the foundation was flooded with requests for the survey to address an array of problems ranging from dangerous railroad crossings to socialist fervor among disaffected immigrants. With so many topics emerging from the community's interest, the foundation board abandoned Fred's initial plan to conduct an all-encompassing municipal study. Instead, over the next decade, the board would choose eight topics they deemed sufficiently compelling to engage a spirited civic debate required to prompt reform. The foundation published its survey findings and presented them in public forums, receiving widespread local press coverage. This work, occurring in the first ten years of the Cleveland Foundation, drove its strategic philanthropy for decades to come. The survey, as a tool for community foundations to engage in thoughtful grant making, has become a common practice for community foundations around the world.

Like Paul Harris and the rapid spread of Rotary across the United States and then the world, Fred's community foundation became a model for cities everywhere. By 1926, more than fifty-five community foundations had been created in cities across the United States. A century later, more than seventeen hundred community foundations currently operate around the world.[54] In 2001, the *Chronicle of Phi-*

---

53 "Groundbreaking Strategy," Cleveland Foundation, accessed March 19, 2024, https://www.clevelandfoundation100.org/foundation-of-change/invention/groundbreaking-strategy/.

54 "An Idea Whose Time Had Come."

lanthropy cited the inception of the Cleveland Foundation as one of ten seminal events that shaped the nonprofit world in the twentieth century. Interestingly, many community foundations—like the one in my hometown, the Coastal Community Foundation of South Carolina—were established by the local Rotary.

When you consider the Cleveland Foundation, Fred's vision of a perpetual, volunteer, and unpaid board of directors drawn from the community the nonprofit serves, with term limits as to the number of years any one director may hold office—that is the quintessential model of contemporary nonprofit governance. His focus on a public nonprofit that was designed to hold significant endowments, whose income is to be deployed to address the problems of the community in which the nonprofit resides, was cutting edge a hundred years ago. But what made this so revolutionary was that the Cleveland Foundation became a vehicle that allowed anyone to be a philanthropist. It gave every individual in the community the ability to contribute to a permanent endowment. Philanthropy was no longer limited to the super wealthy, like the Rockefellers or the Carnegies. Unlike a private foundation, a community foundation enables an entire community to participate in philanthropy as a partnership to address local issues of the day.

Today, the Cleveland Foundation boasts assets of $3 billion and makes grants annually in excess of $130 million.[55] Consider the effect of this much philanthropic power being generated in a grassroots model, accessible to anyone. This creation is the product of the foresight of one philanthropist, Fred Goff, who in my eyes was deeply rooted in the philanthropic way.

---

55 "Impact Investing," Cleveland Foundation, accessed March 19, 2024, https://www. clevelandfoundation.org/grants/impact-investing/.

CHAPTER 10

Evaluating Nonprofit Organizations

P art 3 of this handbook is designed to teach you to evaluate nonprofit organizations as target beneficiaries of your philanthropic plan. Part 3 is written from the perspective that modern American *public charities*, like the Cleveland Foundation, and *private foundations*, like the Rockefeller Foundation, remain the best vehicles in the United States to endow funds and assets for a charitable purpose, with the highest probability that the endowment will remain in place for decades, centuries, or even longer following your passing from this world. Fred Goff's governance model has proven tremendously effective and influential in the design of the modern American nonprofit organization.

At this juncture in the handbook, we need to be clear. There are many ways in which you can be philanthropic. Making charitable gifts to a nonprofit organization is just one way. You can be philanthropic by creating or contributing to knowledge, art, technology, space travel, or really any advancement that benefits humankind. Inherent in philanthropy is the idea that we are endowed with the world into which we are born. A moral obligation of the philanthropist is to leave humanity in a better position when we pass from this existence than when we came into it.

As you read part 3, you may view these lessons either to help you advance your own public charity or private foundation or to evaluate those same nonprofits as grantees or grantors. Whether you're a director, officer, staff, or volunteer, part 3 contains information to help you evaluate your nonprofit organization with objective and subjective metrics that assess the trajectory of your organization.

Organizational Learning and Institutional Knowledge

Just like Fred Goff and the Cleveland Foundation or Paul Harris and Rotary, for every nonprofit organization, there exists at least one philanthropist behind the scenes in pursuit of a philanthropic plan. While guidance on the establishment of a nonprofit organization is beyond the scope of this handbook, suffice it to say that we acknowledge the initial entrepreneurial relationship between the philanthropist and the nonprofit. With each organization that you engage, you should have a sense of its history and how your involvement might integrate into a web of preexisting philanthropic plans and relationships.

As philanthropists, how do we know whether a charity will succeed? Whether our contributions might continue to make an impact long after we are gone? As we take our philanthropic plan toward execution, our ability to evaluate nonprofits becomes critical to its success.

Nonprofit organizations are created predominantly to exist in perpetuity. The starting point of nonprofits is often the same: they are creatures of state law, formed with little variation among board structures and governance models. Many organizations don't succeed and eventually dissolve or are abandoned. A few organizations stand the test of time and continue to exist for decades, even centuries after they were formed. Why?

I see those organizations that survive in the long run as having two skill sets embedded into their governance model. They all have developed a sophisticated system of *organizational learning* that is complemented by an equally sophisticated ability to memorialize *institutional knowledge*. I believe Fred Goff was thinking in these terms when he designed the first community foundation.

Organizational learning exists in environments where there is true leadership and a culture that fosters dialogue around purpose and mission. As the organization learns to capitalize on its institutional knowledge, the organization will track it, record it in the form of bylaws, policies, and other *written* internal controls, and teach successive leaders from one generation to the next these lessons learned. These are essential characteristics of a successful nonprofit. In the case of the Cleveland Foundation, for its first ten years the board engaged in organizational learning as it researched eight different survey topics. The publication of the surveys to the general public as hard-copy books is an example of memorializing institutional knowledge. As simple as it seems, this activity helped drive the grant-making strategy of the Cleveland Foundation in the first half of the twentieth century and became an approach used over and over through the years.

What Is the Standard to Measure a Nonprofit?

Nonprofits that have cultures of organizational learning and the ability to retain institutional knowledge will begin to consider their perpetual existence. Indeed, such an inquiry is foundational for a fiduciary of a nonprofit and, in all cases, leads the organization to consider its accomplishments in terms of "*intergenerational equity.*"

Let us be clear from the outset—I believe the *calculation of the rise or fall of intergenerational equity of a nonprofit organization* is the greatest metric to provide insight to a philanthropist regarding any nonprofit's performance over time.

While the concept of "intergenerational equity" carries with it many dimensions, which we will explore in this handbook, intergenerational equity is, at its core, a mathematical assessment of a nonprofit organization's purchasing power over time. Intergenerational equity in an organization either increases at a rate faster than inflation—and thus the organization has more resources to support its programs—or alternatively, intergenerational equity decreases, and the organization can afford less and less of its programs from one generation to the next. In 1974, the Yale economist James Tobin spoke of intergenerational equity as the ideal investment goal in connection with endowments and their management:

> The trustees of endowed institutions are the guardians of the future against the claims of the present. Their task in managing the endowment is to preserve equity among generations.[56]

I believe the growth of intergenerational equity in a nonprofit organization may only occur when the organization has achieved a high level of organizational learning and can turn that learning into institutional knowledge.

The history of humanity is marked with periods where future generations either receive benefits and accumulated wealth or pay the

---

56 J. Tobin, "What Is Permanent Endowment Income?" *American Economic Review*, 64(2) (1974): 427–432.

debts and transgressions of prior generations. The foresight meditation where we contemplate the origin of a simple screw holding together a chair demonstrates a profound accumulation of intergenerational equity to humankind. Consider that the world around you is really the endowment of those who came before.

Our history has also been marked with periods of setback. The Middle Ages were also known as the Dark Ages for a reason. In the United States, the large increase in government debt being left by the current generations can be viewed as a massive reduction in intergenerational equity for future generations of Americans. It's arguable that such accumulation of debt for current purposes is robbing wealth from future generations. Philanthropists can reverse these trends by amassing assets in a stewardship model that increases intergenerational equity from one generation to the next. The same is true of the environment and our natural resources.

According to one study, "intergenerational equity is a notion that views the human community as a partnership among all generations. Each generation has the right to inherit the same diversity in natural, cultural, health, and economic resources enjoyed by previous generations and to equitable access to the use and benefits of these resources."[57] It is here where the goals embodied in a philanthropist's plan may begin to parallel the long-term strategic plans of an organization looking to endow its programs and services forever.

While there are many objective and subjective measures inherent to intergenerational equity, the calculation causes us to ask: Are organizational resources increasing over time and outpacing inflation, or is the organization losing wealth? Can the nonprofit organization accumulate

---

57 J. K. Summers and L. M. Smith, "The Role of Social and Intergenerational Equity in Making Changes in Human Well-Being Sustainable," *Ambio, 43(6) (October 2014): 718–28,* https://www.ncbi.nlm.nih.gov/pmc/articles/PMC4165836/.

enough wealth to grow its programs and charitable missions? Does the organization have a target size or scale in which it hopes to operate? As philanthropists, we should be conscious of ways in which we may help maturing organizations accumulate intergenerational equity, and we should be drawn to those organizations that are increasing their purchasing power over time.

Assessment of NPOs

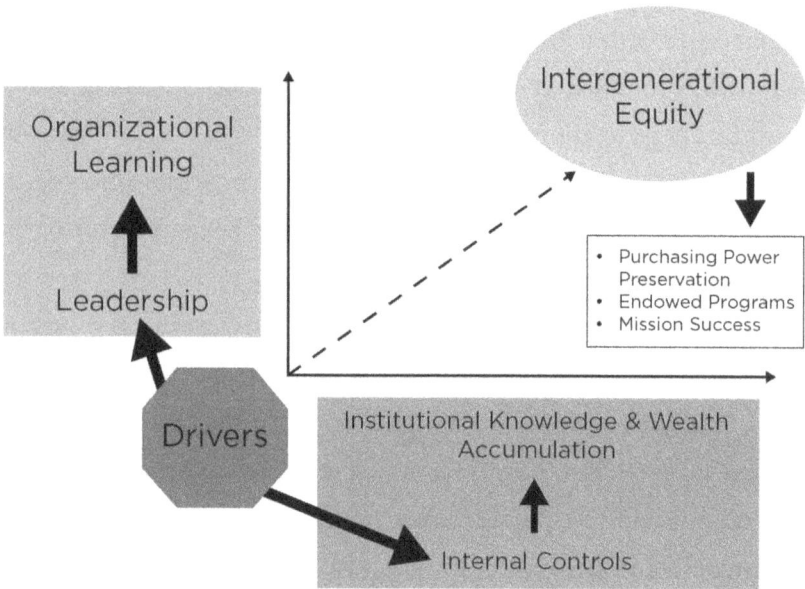

CHAPTER 11

Assessing Organizational Learning—Nonprofit Leadership

Leadership is fundamental to a nonprofit organization's ability to engage in organizational learning.

Leadership in a nonprofit is supported through its governance structure, defined roles, performance expectations, and accountability.

Leadership engages in succession planning such that the organization cultivates talent from within or establishes a culture that attracts quality professionals to fill its ranks.

What Are the Leadership Roles of a Nonprofit?

The absence of private ownership in modern nonprofit organizations creates the necessity for self-perpetuating leadership. The successful nonprofit defines the roles of its leadership structure in a binary manner.

There is a chief executive officer who manages the day-to-day operations, and there is a board of directors that provides oversight to the CEO, approves the operating budget, establishes strategic direction, and is the ultimate authority of the organization. A well-run nonprofit reflects this division of responsibility in all aspects of its governance. The board does not get into the weeds of day-to-day operations or provide oversight to the staff the CEO manages. Likewise, the CEO must recognize the authority of the board and be accountable to that body. The board establishes the strategic vision of the organization, while the CEO executes on that vision by managing the employees and the programs of the organization.

In terms of legal relationships, the CEO is always an employee of the organization, while the board, in the aggregate, exercises the employer role. That means that the board, as a collective, exercises the role of employer—*not* any individual director. There is one exception to this concept. The voice of the board is expressed through its chair. I heard it best expressed that the role of the chair is to "encourage" the CEO. The root of the word *encourage* is "courage," which derives from the Latin word meaning "heart." To encourage someone is to put your heart into that person.

An important indicator of a successful nonprofit organization is the relationship between a CEO and a board chair. Ideally these two individuals will meet frequently. The chair can serve as a mentor, a soundboard, and a cheerleader for the CEO. If the board has determined that there are deficiencies in the performance of a CEO, the chair is best positioned to deliver that message, work on an improvement plan, and check on progress along the way.

When considering a donation to a nonprofit, when all other considerations check out, you might try taking the CEO and the chair to lunch. Watch them to see if they give each other room to speak. Watch how they interact. Are they respectful to each other? Or do they step on each other's sentences? Does one dominate the conversation, or do they share time to speak? This is an informal barometer to determine how well a nonprofit might be operating or falling into dysfunction.

Other factors that come into play are whether the board does an annual performance review of its CEO. Performance review metrics should be designed to emphasize areas of improvement and align compensation with outcomes. Ideally, the board will present to the CEO the format and questions related to the performance review at the start of the year. This format can serve as a guide between the CEO and the chair during the year. If it's customized and thoughtful, the format of the performance review itself will drive performance of the CEO (and the board). There should be periodic check-ins during the year to ensure that everyone is on track. At the conclusion of the year, each director may be invited to provide an individualized assessment based on the review format. The chair can aggregate such reports as a tool to present to the CEO for further engagement. This is how leadership excels in a nonprofit. This is how you optimize the relationship between the board and the CEO.

There is also a limit to this relationship. The board must empower the CEO to manage the staff of the nonprofit. Directors are advised not to overstep the CEO by engaging directly with employees who otherwise report to and are under the supervision of the CEO. If the culture of an organization enables a staff person to jump-skip the CEO to seek favor of individual directors, such a break in the chain of command will spread like a cancer across the body of the organization. It will undermine both the current CEO's and future CEOs' authority to manage staff. Of course, there's a balance between management of human resources and the memorialized policies for handling griev-ances and whistleblowing when fraud, theft, harassment, crime, or other serious issues might arise. In those cases, it is appropriate for an employee to seek the counsel of the board. However, there should be protocols in place (i.e., written internal controls) accessible to everyone in the organization to assist employees in responding to these rare but significant issues.

A CEO should not be a member of the board or governing body. CEOs may and should be invited to attend all board meetings, but their inclusion as a director on the board will create continuing conflicts of interest across all manner of board business, including performance oversight of the organization and the CEO. Such a crossover will blur the push-pull characteristics associated with a budget-approving board versus the CEO in charge of implementing programs within the budget. Moreover, if ever you're on a board that must contemplate the discipline or termination of an individual as CEO, you will either appreciate the fact that the CEO is not an ex officio director on your board, or you will realize another example of the problem. If the CEO were the director, you would likely have to give notice to the CEO of the board meeting, including the purpose, and then ask the CEO to recuse herself. That's tricky to navigate in real life.

Succession Planning

Another indicator of an organization engaged in organizational learning is how well the organization approaches succession planning in terms of its board, officers, and staff. While it's often not considered, the committee that manages nominations of individuals to director and officer positions may be the most significant committee in a nonprofit organization. It is through this committee that leadership may be identified or homegrown. A nominating committee is a critical structure that promotes and enhances organizational learning.

An effective nominating committee will develop an ongoing set of criteria or matrix for skill sets and personalities that it would like to imbue in an organization. The nominating committee will review and regularly update such criteria with the board on an annual basis to ensure that the current needs of the board are met in terms of skills, roles, and personality. This process is the means by which a nonprofit may cultivate its own leadership.

Philanthropists are advised to seek those organizations that are creative in their nomination process. These organizations will establish processes and protocols that are rooted in organizational history and often uniquely expressed. For example, I have a nonprofit client that composes its nominating committee entirely of prior board chairs. This organization is creatively involving its predecessor leaders. As former board chairs, these individuals have engaged in that critical relationship with the organization's CEO. They've all worked on a common strategic vision, which is hopefully being passed down from chair to chair. Through the composition of this committee, the organization's institutional knowledge is being retained and used to repopulate the board and officer positions, including each successor chair. It shouldn't surprise you that in 2023, this client cleared $137 million in revenue and pledged gifts.

Governance Committee

In recent years, there has been a trend to house the nominations function in a governance committee tasked with a broader purpose to enhance the ongoing governance of an organization, including reviewing and updating bylaws and policies of the board. When "nominations" are housed within a governance committee, you can see the added benefits of having the committee also handle new-director orientation. A governance committee is also positioned to assess directors' and officers' performance during the year, including attendance at meetings and whether such individuals have contributed financially to the nonprofit. There should be no assumption that when a director's or officer's term of service ends, the board will automatically reelect such individual. A governance or nominating committee should vet reelection similarly to the initial election.

Term Limits

You should also consider whether the nonprofit organization has term limits associated with its director and officer roles. In most cases, having term limits is healthy for the organization. It ensures that the lifeblood of a board refreshes consistently with new perspectives and ideas, giving more people in the community a chance to stand up and serve. This was an important detail for Fred Goff as he conceptualized the Cleveland Foundation.

But sometimes, those individuals who are meeting the call should not be precluded from continued service due to a term limit. These are occasions when a board may want to waive a term limit. An example might be if a term limit arises for a director who is also serving in an officer role. It would be acceptable to waive the term limit for the individual to complete the officer term. Likewise, in a start-up nonprofit, you may prefer to not have term limits altogether until the organization becomes more mature. A future board can always amend the bylaws and impose term limits on service at a later time.

There is one issue with which you should take the utmost care when you don't have term limits: Has any of your leadership caught a case of "*founderitis*"? This is seen when an individual gives themselves the title of "Founder" of the nonprofit. The concept of *founder* does not exist in nonprofit corporate law. Moreover, it seems to connote ownership and ego of the founder over the organization. It begs the question whether the founder is fully putting the interests of the organization ahead of their own and whether the ego of the founder is overcoming their empathy. Founderitis is a contrary force to organizational learning and institutional knowledge and will deter succession planning. As a result, when the founder dies or can no longer serve, that usually means the end of the organization. I've seen this many times. Term limits can be a cure for an organization infected with founderitis.

Annual Director and Officer Pledge

Just as CEOs are provided a format template to assess and review performance, many high-performing nonprofits will require each director and officer to sign an annual pledge to the nonprofit. This pledge may include commitments of financial support, confidentiality, and disclosure of conflicts of interest, but the pledge can cover more expansive matters, such as codes of conduct, agreements to attend meetings, expectations of civility at meetings, and awareness of how one's presence in the community may reflect on the nonprofit. Managing expectations helps create a culture of accountability, which in turn leads to a certain self-awareness in an organization. At least once a year, directors and officers might be asked to acknowledge these expectations. The goal here is to remind leadership in a nonprofit that mission must always precede personal interest.

These practices enable organizational learning in its highest form, and when reduced to writing, they become a part of the institutional knowledge of the nonprofit. Organizations that seek creative ways to gather, retain, and pass on knowledge are the ones with the highest probability to succeed and be sustainable.

Leadership Reflection

Let's use our philanthropic skills of empathy and foresight to envision the perspectives of an organization's CEO and board chair.

Each individual and organization is unique. Whether you look at individuals from a Myers-Briggs personality assessment or in terms of astrological signs, no specific cookie-cutter type owns the role of leader. Leaders emerge from all socioeconomic backgrounds, cultures, families, and life experiences. CEOs and board chairs are the leaders of their organizations. Whether they can lead as a team is the difference between success or regression.

The CEO of a nonprofit is a professional who functions as the highest-ranking employee of the organization. When taking this job, the CEO knows they will never be an owner or possess equity in the organization the way they might in a for-profit company. Motivation of an individual who aspires to be the CEO of a nonprofit organization will vary from person to person and industry to industry. The CEO of a health system will be very different from a counterpart at a college or museum or food bank or homeless shelter or advocacy group, and on and on. Most CEOs will be intuitively attracted to the nonprofit's mission—how the organization may fit into society and what problems it will seek to address.

Let's focus on the role of CEO as an employee. Based on what you've learned, how important is the annual performance review? How much angst might a CEO have when the board is considering nominees to director and officer positions? How involved might the CEO be in such board succession planning? Is the CEO granted input in the succession planning of the board chair? Not all personalities are a match. If the CEO has been in that role for a long time, what's it like to have the role of the chair, the singular voice and expression of the board, change with a high degree of frequency? Does a CEO have an interest in the term length of the chair role? Is one year too short, or should a chair be able to occupy that seat for two, three, or four years? As you review an organization, consider the perspective of its CEO.

Where do board chairs come from? They are usually volunteers from the community who have a passion for the mission of the organization. While some chairs are serial volunteers, many are rooted in a for-profit perspective, and their prior business experience may not always translate well. If the board chair is a CEO of a for-profit in their day job, will they exert that perspective on the CEO of the nonprofit, or will they be able to act in a support and oversight role to the CEO? As the CEO of the nonprofit manages and leads the staff, can the board chair serve in a complementary capacity with the other directors of the board? Can the chair maintain discipline over the board to restrain the urge to cross the line into the day-to-day operations of the CEO and staff?

Let's turn our visualization to the perspective of the chair. Unlike the CEO, the chair is not (and should not be) an employee of the nonprofit. The time and knowledge of the chair is a donation in kind, unvalued but immeasurably valuable. How does the chair relate to the CEO? How frequently do they meet?

Let's reenvision ourselves finally as being on the nominating committee, tasked to identify successor chairs and CEOs. Consider the questions that arise in evaluating an individual's potential to fill a specific role. Consider the individual relationships that might mesh or conflict. Where do you begin? How might you evoke empathy to step into the perspectives of the individuals seated as CEO and chair?

Based on the foregoing, what insights do you have to manifest foresight and pair the optimal leaders together?

Maturation of Organizational Learning

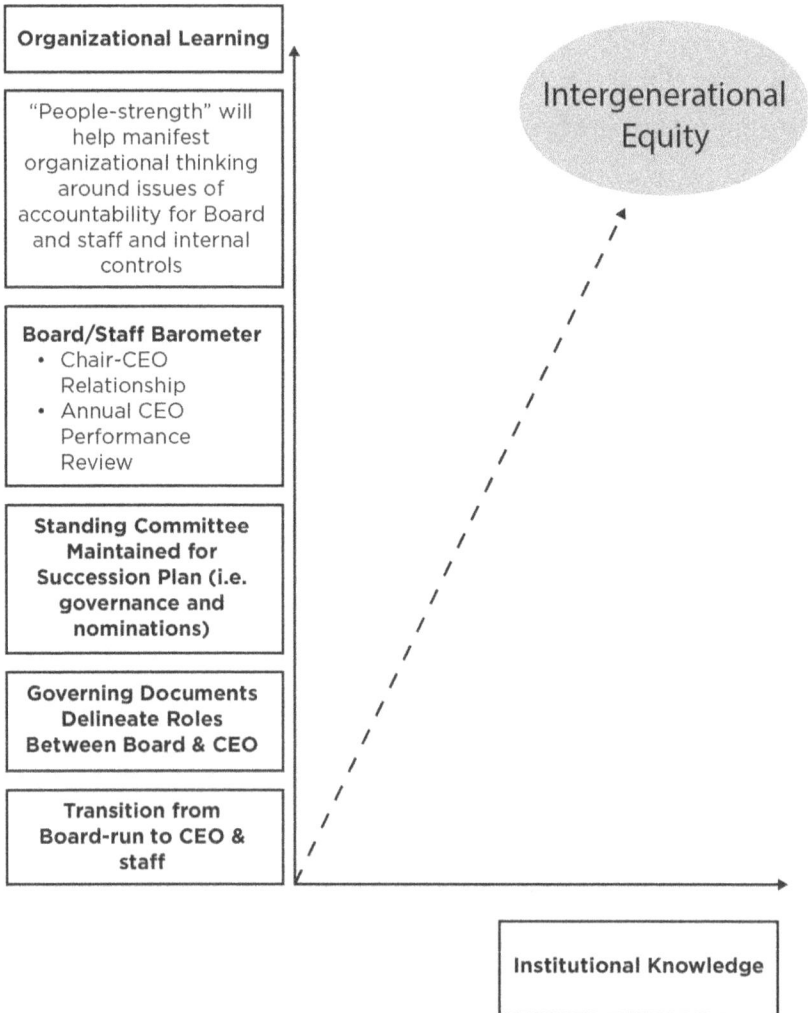

Organizational Learning

"People-strength" will help manifest organizational thinking around issues of accountability for Board and staff and internal controls

Board/Staff Barometer
- Chair-CEO Relationship
- Annual CEO Performance Review

Standing Committee Maintained for Succession Plan (i.e. governance and nominations)

Governing Documents Delineate Roles Between Board & CEO

Transition from Board-run to CEO & staff

Intergenerational Equity

Institutional Knowledge

CHAPTER 12

Assessing Institutional Knowledge—Internal Controls

The absence of stock or other forms of equity ownership in a nonprofit organization heightens the importance of memorialized policies and protocols to manage the activities of the organization, with a particular focus on financial accountability. These policies and protocols are referred to as *internal controls* of an organization.

A hallmark of internal controls is that, in theory, they're not dependent on any specific person. They're adopted by an ever-changing board or governing body with the intent that the controls will exist well into the future. Sophisticated internal controls will be the output of organizational learning of the board.

Internal controls are also a result of effective recordkeeping; consequently, they're a blossoming achievement of institutional knowledge of an organization. Internal controls manifest themselves in the form of articles, bylaws, policies, minutes, and resolutions. Mature nonprofit organizations will maintain repositories of such information, which are accessible to each member of the governing body or appropriate committee. Nowadays, many cloud-based repositories for boards exist, which make it increasingly easy for directors to access all manner of these materials, including archived meeting minutes. A well-run nonprofit will also ask directors and officers to reaffirm their commitment to follow such governing documents and internal controls on a periodic basis.

The following is a nonexhaustive list of internal controls in the form of governing documents and policies:

- Articles or Certificate of Incorporation
- Bylaws
- Conflict of interest policy
- Compensation policy
- Whistleblower policy
- Joint venture policy
- Record retention policy
- Audit policy
- Gift acceptance policy
- Expenditure and signatory authority (reaffirmed annually by the board)
- Donor-oriented policies, such as donor bill of rights and policy on donor information confidentiality
- IT policies, such as security policy and terms of use/privacy policy of a website

Additional indicators of whether an organization is maintaining its institutional knowledge appropriately are the consistent tracking and approval of minutes of meetings of the various governing bodies and the retention of such minutes in the corporate book of the organization. Are minutes taken for each meeting and then approved at the following meeting? Do minutes read like a transcript, or do they merely detail the highlights of each meeting and are sparse on quotes? The latter is preferable.

In addition to the recording of minutes, we can look at how well run board and committee meetings are. Are notices of the meetings sent to attendees in advance based on a preestablished number of days that complies with applicable law and the organization's bylaws? Most state laws require notice for regular meetings of seven to ten days in advance of the meeting. Does the notice have a complete agenda with appropriate read-aheads, like the prior meeting minutes, any motions for consideration, and various reports, like statements of activities, position, and cash flow? Sending these materials twenty-four hours in advance of a meeting is not only ineffective but also wastes the valuable (donated) time of a volunteer board. These are the small things that, cumulatively speaking, are incredibly important. Believe it or not, these types of factors play into whether the organization is generating intergenerational equity. If you can't govern well, you'll get nowhere. Conversely, if everyone sustains a high level of professionalism, it sets a standard for all areas of the organization.

The True Achievement of Accountability

An organization that engages in organizational learning achieves self-awareness through accountability. Accountability needs to be ingrained internally in the governance design of an organization through thoughtful and identifiable checks and balances. These checks and balances should not impede an organization's nimbleness but instead allow for a second set of eyes on all transactions. Accountability is about creating moments of self-assessment regarding financial and operational performance. Accountability also needs to be extramural. Organizations need to be transparent and honest with themselves to allow for an external review. In many ways, accountability might be expressed through multiple alarms that are hardwired into the temporal existence of the organization, set like a clock to remind the nonprofit during the fiscal year to wake up and check on itself.

As a nonprofit matures and its board begins to create standing committees, the finance committee emerges early in the life of an organization. The treasurer often chairs the finance committee, ex officio. In the early stages in the life of a nonprofit, the finance committee might at first be responsible for any audit of the nonprofit.

In engaging an auditor, it's best to consider selecting a third party that is unrelated to the organization and its directors. The selection of the auditor itself is a form of internal control. Given the expense of an audit, initially many organizations seek an audit only once every three or five years.

When an organization reaches a point where it seeks an audit every year, it has hit another significant milestone in maturity. At this point organizations should consider whether to allocate the audit function to an independent audit committee instead of continuing to house that function in the finance committee. If you have different individuals serving on the audit committee who are not involved in the annual budget creation, oversight, and review process, the audit committee will have more objectivity in the performance of its role, which adds value and credence to this oversight process. The treasurer should not be on the audit committee. Again, this is another form of checks and balances.

It's also preferable that the nonprofit engage an independent accounting firm to conduct the audit that neither handles the day-to-day bookkeeping nor prepares the tax returns of the organization. Ideally, the nonprofit should engage two different accounting firms—one for audit and one for accounting/tax preparation. In practice, the audit firm checks the work of the accounting firm. If the audit report renders a clean opinion, then the accounting firm has the clearance to prepare the Form 990 tax return. In this way, tax reporting always follows and relies on the audit function. Check and control.

Lastly, an organization should consider changing third-party auditors on a periodic basis, such as every five years, to diversify review among different professionals with different experiences and training.

Maturation of Institutional Knowledge

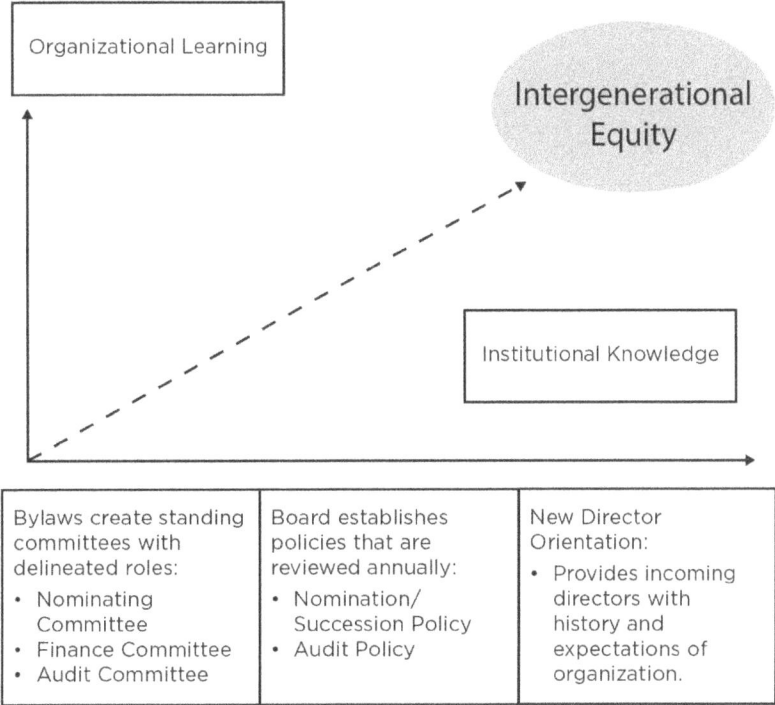

Bylaws create standing committees with delineated roles: • Nominating Committee • Finance Committee • Audit Committee	Board establishes policies that are reviewed annually: • Nomination/ Succession Policy • Audit Policy	New Director Orientation: • Provides incoming directors with history and expectations of organization.

CHAPTER 13

Objective Measures of Nonprofits

A philanthropist who is grounded in the ethics of information and truth should value financial metrics as the means to measure an organization that is pursuing the accumulation of intergenerational equity. If you are looking to create a permanent endowment with an organization pursuant to a significant gift, you have tools to assess the financial strength and internal controls of a nonprofit. That's not the complete picture, but it's a start. For others on a different journey, you might be establishing a new nonprofit organization or serving on a board as part of your philanthropic plan. Use these metrics in those contexts. Include them in your regular reports to your board. You can only meet best practices if you make an effort to respond to what you see and share that knowledge with others, with the goal of memorializing insights in the form of policies, minutes, and records. Boards should be mindful of the power of policy in terms of sharing lessons learned to be passed from one generation to the next.

Reading the Form 990 Tax Return and Audited Financial Statements

If a nonprofit asks you to donate to it or join its board of directors, there are two documents, for which you might ask, that will provide insight into the organization's capacity for organizational learning and memorialization of institutional knowledge. The Form 990 and the audited financial statements are the report cards that may be used to assess these twin capacities of a nonprofit.

FORM 990

The current federal tax return in the United States for nonprofit organizations is the Form 990. There is no greater tool to gain a line of sight into an organization than the Form 990. This is particularly true if you can see several years of consecutive returns.

The Form 990 tax return was used for the first time in 1941. It was only two pages. Today's form, with all the schedules completed, can exceed hundreds of pages for robust endowment foundations. It's more aptly described as an "informational" return. This is because of the number of questions that require narrative answers or that probe into the organization's governance practices, including whether the nonprofit has adopted conflict of interest, compensation, whistleblower, record retention, and joint venture policies.

AUDITED FINANCIAL STATEMENTS

Many nonprofits conduct significant prep work in anticipation of the submission of the Form 990. This is done in accordance with board policies, with the governing board seeking to engage the auditor at the *start* of the new fiscal year to review the year prior. The board will ask the auditor to compare and confirm the *Statement of Activi-*

ties, which is the nonprofit version of a profit/loss statement, and the *Statement of Position*, which is the nonprofit version of a balance sheet, against the books, records, and accounts of the nonprofit for the applicable time period. The auditor will review the effectiveness of the staff's compliance with internal controls, test donor pledges for reliability, and examine the financial strengths and weaknesses of the organization. If the auditor determines that the nonprofit is in serious trouble, the auditor will indicate that the nonprofit is a "*going concern*," which, contrary to the sound of the term, means the organization lacks enough funds to be sustainable both in the short and long run. It is poised for bankruptcy.

FINANCIAL METRICS ARISING OUT OF THE FORM 990 AND AUDITED FINANCIAL STATEMENTS

While this handbook challenges the reader to consider subjective measurements of nonprofit success around organizational learning and institutional knowledge, there are also objective metrics of assessment you can draw from a nonprofit's tax return and financial statements.

Provided here is a list of metrics for your consideration as you evaluate the landscape of nonprofit organizations as potential beneficiaries of your philanthropic goals. As you consider these metrics, please note that these are ideals of nonprofit performance. We should expect a mature organization with a sizeable endowment to meet or exceed the following metrics. However, many more nonprofits are thriving in much earlier stages of maturation. You may be inspired to help these earlier-stage nonprofits along the way. In some instances, a poor metric in one area may create an opportunity for targeted charitable support or volunteer engagement.

1. Stewardship Ratio

The Statement of Activities of an organization can reveal a *stewardship ratio*, which reflects the efficiency of the organization in delivering its programmatic services. If you take the "*total program services*" line of a Statement of Activities and divide it by the aggregate "*total expenses*," you will see a ratio that reflects how well the management of the organization stewards funds in relation to programmatic output. This ratio can tell donors, for each donated dollar, how much the organization will spend on mission versus administrative overhead.

For example, if a nonprofit spent $725,000 in total program services related to total expenses of $1,010,000, you would see a stewardship ratio of 71 percent.

I've listened to many auditors and advisors indicate that a target stewardship ratio for a nonprofit organization should be 85 percent. If the ratio is higher than 85 percent, that indicates the staff of the nonprofit may be overtaxed in their workload. There is likely under-compensation in relation to efforts, potential for low morale, and the possibility of burnout and loss of talent. If you go past 90 percent, the organization may be overheating and near a meltdown, which could set it back significantly in its maturation. While I share the concern about burnout when the stewardship ratio starts to exceed 85 or 90 percent—and I can't stress enough the importance for a board to step in under those circumstances—I'm not certain that 85 percent is a correct rule of thumb in terms of a target stewardship ratio for the entire nonprofit sector.

Based on my experience having reviewed thousands of audited financial statements over the years, I find that most effective organizations are operating at a stewardship ratio closer to 70 to 75 percent. I also think that in the real world, a wide variety of stewardship ratios are perfectly fine. The appropriate stewardship ratio depends on the mission of the nonprofit, its industry niche, the market in which it serves, and potentially a number of other factors.

I don't believe in a generic stewardship ratio that applies to all nonprofits.

In a recent study where 22,328 US arts and cultural nonprofits, largely museums and theaters, were examined from 2008 to 2018, the results demonstrated a sweet spot in terms of stewardship ratio for this industry.[58] The study measured success by the number of people going to the museum or theater for an exhibit or performance. They found that when an arts organization devoted 35 percent of its budget to overhead, the organization did the best in terms of attendance. Interestingly, nonprofits that spent below that threshold saw attendance decline by 9 percent, and conversely, those that spent way too much fell by as much as 30 percent. This data appears to support the notion that for nonprofit theaters and museums, a stewardship ratio of 65 percent may be the sweet spot.

A challenge for the nonprofit sector is to dispel the myth that nonprofit overhead takes away from mission. It's not realistic for donors to demand that overhead be less than 5, 10, or even 15 percent. A stewardship ratio of 85 percent is just not reasonable. Donors who exert pressure to starve a nonprofit into high performance fail to recognize that every job in a nonprofit contributes to mission. Starving a nonprofit can result in loss of talent, replacing paid professional staff with volunteers, or being forced to use outdated facilities and equipment. This is not how long-term value is built in a nonprofit.

---

58 "Nonprofits May Need to Spend about One-Third of Their Budget on Overhead to Thrive—Contradicting a Rule of Thumb for Donors," The Conversation, September 19, 2022, https://theconversation.com/nonprofits-may-need-to-spend-about-one-third-of-their-budget-on-overhead-to-thrive-contradicting-a-rule-of-thumb-for-donors-188792.

As philanthropists, let's tap into our ethic of information and truth and consider the importance of the stewardship ratio as a significant tool to assess an organization. When you review a nonprofit's stewardship ratio, you might first seek comparative data from industry peers to consider an industry-wide target.

If you are serving on a board of directors, I challenge you to consider taking up the following question: **What is the ideal stewardship ratio of my organization that, if continuously hit, results in the greatest programmatic results, married with the highest possible job satisfaction of staff?** When you think about it, that is a powerful question for a board to consider.

When a board reviews industry peers to determine an aspirational stewardship ratio for its organization, the result is a metric that assesses not only the financial strength and efficiency of the organization but also its staff satisfaction. When a board does this, it is articulating the organization's cultural values and identity. Being able to express this deeper thought around an articulated target stewardship ratio is key for a nonprofit to establish itself as a viable champion and partner for philanthropists. Should a development officer be asked about overhead costs of the nonprofit, isn't it a better conversation for the development officer to be able to describe the board's strategic process to determine its ideal stewardship ratio? Won't that demonstrate to the donor prospect that the nonprofit engages in a high level of organizational learning and retention of institutional knowledge? Isn't this type of conversation a foundation for trust between the donor and the nonprofit?

2. Reserve Ratio

Another measure of financial health is to divide the total value of unrestricted net assets by the total monthly expenses. Should the number be less than 1.0, then the nonprofit is unlikely to meet its obligations within the next thirty days. The ideal reserve ratio for the nonprofit will be 6.0. When you consider the math, this ratio essentially indicates whether the nonprofit has amassed a six-month operating reserve as savings for rainy days.

Once an organization has achieved its reserve ratio, it's likely in a position to consider the establishment of one or more endowments for the funding of programs or operations. This is a significant milestone toward intergenerational equity. Prior to achieving a six-month reserve, a nonprofit may not have the financial strength to permanently restrict funds toward a specific purpose. If an organization pursues the establishment of an endowment too early in its maturation, you will see a conflict in the organization between fundraising for immediate general operations and growing an endowment for the future. Immediate needs should come first.

3. Quick Ratio

To test a Statement of Position (i.e., the balance sheet) and understand the true liquidity of an organization to meet its current obligation, you can take the total cash and cash equivalents on a Statement of Position and divide that number by the total liabilities, also known as the *quick ratio*. Many banks use the quick-ratio comparison to gauge financial stability. It compares quick assets (current assets less inventory and prepaid expenses) to current liabilities. Your organization's quick ratio should not be less than 1.0. Again, that signals that the nonprofit may not be able to meet its current financial obligations. A number higher than 1.0 reflects the strength in liquidity of a nonprofit but remember that once your cash on hand results in a reserve ratio of 6.0 or better, as fiduciaries the board should start to consider where to place such funds in order to create some sort of return. You can see how success can naturally lead a nonprofit toward the establishment of an endowment.

4. Fundraising Efficiency

Do you know how much you're generating from fundraising activities? This ratio indicates the amount of contributions that result from fundraising expenses. To calculate, you divide the total charitable contributions by the total fundraising expenses. When fundraising generates a multiple of nine times or greater the expense invested in fundraising, the organization is operating at very efficient levels. When you don't see that type of return, it is time to reflect on what is going wrong. Is it a messaging issue, a person issue, a lack of board engagement, or some combination of factors?

In the early stages of a nonprofit, this leverage must rise quickly and consistently. Typically, it is the founding board that engages in the first major financial lift of the entity. If their work is successful, the board can hire its first staff person. This is the moment when the nonprofit achieves the binary model of governance, balanced between a board of directors and a chief executive officer/staff. Interestingly, I have found that the first hire of a nonprofit organization is often not a CEO but instead is frequently a development officer whose primary responsibility is fundraising.

5. Operating Margin

This is an important forecasting ratio because it illustrates an organization's ability to produce a potential surplus that the board may draw on if needed in future years. To calculate, you subtract total expenditures from total revenues and divide that sum by total revenues. This percentage is your operating margin. It is what's left over after your organization has paid all its bills. It is with operating margin, over time, that a nonprofit can amass an appropriate reserve ratio and then transition to the establishment of one or more endowments.

6. Operating Reliance

To show how much an organization can pay for total expenses solely from program revenues, you divide total program revenues by total program expenses. If you have a number less than one, you are operating your program in the red. Revenue from other sources like fundraising is required to keep the program afloat. The concept of operating reliance can cause a board to reflect on the viability and importance of a specific program. This information may inform a board or a CEO when it is time to sunset a program. However, an understanding of operating reliance can inspire or acknowledge the need for a fundraising component for survival of the program. From an intergenerational equity perspective, awareness of operating reliance issues enables a board to reflect on how much corpus will need to be raised and then restricted in an endowment to kick off enough income to run the applicable program of the nonprofit.

7. Change in Net Assets

This metric measures financial performance by answering the question "Did your organization live within its means during the year?" While an organization's success shouldn't be judged by whether it had a positive or negative change in net assets from one year to the next, consecutive deficits should be cause for concern. Is a negative change the result of poor performance in the markets lowering the value of your endowments? Has a major donor passed away or otherwise moved on? Was a program unsuccessful? Was there an unbudgeted liability? These are the questions that need to be addressed when a negative trend in the value of net assets emerges in an organization's tax returns and audited financial statements. However, when you see the trend moving upward over many years, that's a pretty good sign that the nonprofit is gaining intergenerational equity. But there is a caveat on this last point. To gain intergenerational equity, the rate of growth must exceed the rate of inflation over the same period. If it doesn't, while the change in net assets may be positive, the purchasing power is decreasing due to inflation. In such a case, the nonprofit is losing intergenerational equity, but it may not be as obvious to see.

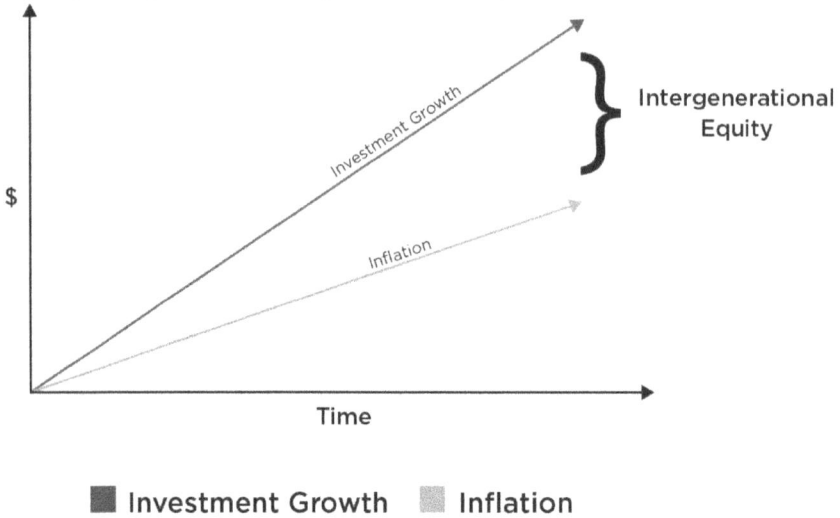

The Value of Metrics

Ideally, a nonprofit organization with one or more endowments will have a reserve ratio of 6.0 or greater, representing rainy-day cash on hand to pay all expenses in the ordinary course for the next six months. This will ensure a strong viability ratio, current ratio, and quick ratio. Annually, there should be adequate funds from the operating margin that the organization may itself contribute to an endowment. If your organization is not operating at this level, then your organization's current financial needs will likely exceed its ability to establish an endowment.

Your organization's fundraising returns should be a multiple of your fundraising expenses. Many think that should be nine or greater. You should watch your fundraising return in relation to your reliance on operating revenue for your programs to remain open. While you always want your programs to pay for themselves, the board will expect fundraising to close any gap. You can also see that there is a correlation to the amount of income an endowment may be expected to return and the cost to run a program that otherwise operates at a loss.

Year to year, you should be watching the stewardship ratio for your industry to ensure that you are expending funds efficiently while not burning out staff or volunteers. Changes in net assets from year to year, particularly with the endowment base, will give you a line of sight into whether intergenerational equity is growing or shrinking. Be mindful that the percentage change in net assets of your endowment from year to year needs to exceed any increase of inflation for the same period of time.

Nonprofit Assessment of Ability to Start an Endowment

Metric	Formula	Notes	Target Calculation
Stewardship Ratio	Total program services divided by total expenses.	TBD by the board based on comparative industry data.	70%-75%
Reserve Ratio	Total value of unrestricted net assets divided by total monthly expenses.	Must never go below 1.	6.0 or greater
Quick Ratio	Total cash and cash equivalents divided by total liabilities.	Must never go below 1. Target ratio will depend on your ability to liquidate short-term investments. If you hold deferred programmatic revenue, this formula is a quick check to confirm that you have not expended such revenue prematurely.	3.0-6.0
Fundraising Efficiency	Total charitable contributions divided by the total fundraising expenses.		9
Operating Margin		TBD by the board in terms of profitability of programs and fundraising. At a minimum, this should be an amount that equals or exceeds inflation.	Amount to exceed Consumer Price Index for that year.
Operating Reliance	Divide total program revenues by total program expenses.	Used to assess whether a program breaks even or requires fundraising support.	TBD by the board based on importance of program to mission.
Change in Net Assets		This is an indicator of intergenerational equity. At a minimum, this should be an amount that equals or exceeds inflation.	Rate of growth to exceed Consumer Price Index for that year.

CHAPTER 14

Why Are Philanthropists Attracted to Endowments?

For the philanthropist aiming to make a difference for as many generations as possible, the establishment or funding of an "*endowment*" may be one of the most meaningful accomplishments. It's for good reason that donors often establish or fund endowments through planned gifts.

For many English-speaking Americans, when they hear the word *endow*, they recall the Declaration of Independence, where Thomas Jefferson wrote, "We hold these truths to be self-evident, that all men are created equal, that they are endowed by their Creator with certain unalienable Rights, that among these are Life, Liberty and the pursuit of Happiness."

The foundation of the great American experiment can't be better encapsulated than by those words: *life, liberty, and the pursuit of happiness*. The Founding Fathers believed those words represented inherent rights of all human beings. Just as we are endowed with the human form, so too are we endowed with rights. While the Founding Fathers captured the top three for Americans, they also recognized that life, liberty, and the pursuit of happiness are part of a nonexhaustive list. One might view the culture wars that have raged from time to time in the American experience as the ongoing exploration of what our society and its collective conscious views as unalienable rights.

The word *endow* itself originates from the Latin *dotare*, which means to give. It evolved across the European languages into a variety of progeny, including the old French word *douer*, meaning to provide an income for, which was also foundational in the emergence of the word *dowry* in English. When *ment* was added to *endow* in the late 1500s, we began using *endowment* to indicate a gift given to a public institution.

In modern vernacular, an endowment is an established fund of cash, securities, investments, or other assets that a nonprofit invests to generate income. The expenditure of such income is restricted to specific uses or types of programs, assets, or activities of the nonprofit. Most endowments are established with permanent restrictions, although some are temporarily restricted. Permanently restricted endowments forbid expenditures of the principal or corpus of the gift. The nonprofit is required to invest the corpus in perpetuity. The nonprofit may also be required to spend some portion of the income from the endowment each year for the nonprofit's operations. These are the characteristics that attract donors to endowments.

The Uniform Prudent Management of Institutional Funds Act (UPMIFA) is a template body of law that provides guidance on investment decisions and endowment expenditures for nonprofit organizations regarding their endowments and institutional funds. This body of law creates a framework for nonprofit compliance when managing an endowment that should provide assurances to donors. States began to enact various versions of UPMIFA between 2008 and 2010, largely in response to issues that arose during the Great Recession. The predecessor to UPMIFA, called the Uniform Management of Institutional Funds Act (UMIFA), was approved by the National Conference of Commissioners on Uniform State Laws in 1972. As of 2008, forty-seven states had adopted some version of UMIFA.[59]

Under UMIFA, a nonprofit can spend any appreciation above the historic dollar value of an endowment (i.e., the original donated amount), but nothing below that threshold. In the United States, during the years immediately following the 2008 financial crisis, non-profits with sizable endowments were unable to release enough funds from their endowments to stave off bankruptcy. UPMIFA changed the law by adding a *P* for *prudent*. This change acknowledged nuance and context in the exercise of fiduciary responsibility. However, this change increased the ability of a nonprofit to seek a court's assistance to modify donor restrictions associated with an endowment, particularly to stave off bankruptcy and potentially save the nonprofit. Fred Goff would appreciate this change of law to help loosen the dead hand of the philanthropist. It only took a century following the incorporation of the Cleveland Foundation for UPMIFA to be enacted.

Establishing Endowments

From a donor's perspective, making a gift into an endowment may better align with the level of impact that most donors seek. If left to do its own thing for long enough, the income thrown off from an endowment can exceed the original amount donated. Remember from part 1 the Benjamin Franklin charitable trusts in Boston and

---

59　While there is a standard framework to UPMIFA, each state has the ability, which many have exercised, to change the terms of the statutory framework. For our purposes, we will only speak to that found in the model act. Each philanthropist is therefore advised to confirm the terms of the version of UPMIFA adopted by their state or the state in which the donee nonprofit is situated.

Philadelphia, which have funded city projects for more than two hundred years. Consider the annual distribution of the Cleveland Foundation today of $130 million.

A philanthropist should know the difference between an *endowment* and a *quasi-endowment*. A quasi-endowment is a form of an endowment that the board of the nonprofit establishes. The board acts as the donor. While the composition of a board may change, the board will continue to exist as long as the organization does. In that way, the board is always in place and may amend or remove the restrictions from the quasi-endowment, including the ability to later expend principal. This is the greatest risk for an external donor when making a gift to a quasi-endowment. At any point, the nonprofit board may unwind such a quasi-endowment at its absolute discretion. That said, a quasi-endowment is a good starting place for nonprofit boards as they consider the creation of their nonprofit's first endowment. It allows the board to learn as it goes and make changes before it agrees to convert a quasi-endowment to an endowment, which is an option as well.

By contrast, an endowment is established by a nonprofit board and an external donor pursuant to a gift agreement that both parties sign. Thus the gift becomes a binding contract to the nonprofit in the truest sense, enforceable in a court of law. Absent a compelling showing under UPMIFA, mutual agreement of the parties is typically required to amend a true endowment. Absent donor consent, a nonprofit board does not have unilateral ability to unwind an endowment. This presents some practical problems after a donor dies.

You should also be mindful whether you're creating a new endowment or providing funds to an existing endowment of a nonprofit. By pouring funds into a true endowment, you will also gain the ability to enforce the existing restrictions in the endowment.

In theory, the greater the number of philanthropists who contribute to the same endowment, the greater the number of societal protections that will imbue into that endowment.

We have explored intergenerational equity as the measure of a nonprofit organization's performance over time. In the endowment context, we measure intergenerational equity when we examine whether the endowment's return exceeds inflation. In this way, we can measure whether the nonprofit is able to expend funds equally in relation to current and future generations or whether the purchasing power of the endowment is declining. When intergenerational equity rises, in theory, inefficiencies, disparities, and injustices in capitalism shrink. A review of changes in intergenerational equity of an endowment over time will help a philanthropist evaluate the nonprofit managers' performance. This is the true test of whether the managers of an endowment have met their fiduciary obligations. Has intergenerational equity associated with an endowment grown, remained flat, or shrunk over the years?

Internal Controls around Endowments

To manage an endowment, current boards must be able to share knowledge with future boards. There are two primary endowment policies through which a nonprofit board may convey experience and information:

- Investment policy statement
- Spending policy

A successful nonprofit organization focused on increasing its sustainability and purchasing power will memorialize its goals and strategy in its investment policy statement (IPS). The board should regularly review the IPS against market conditions and needs of the nonprofit. An IPS should be a living document that receives a high degree of engagement from the board.

Similarly, the spending policy should be focused on the needs of the organization for cash into the future. Typically, spending policies target an annual payout of 3 to 4 percent of the assets of an endowment. The spending rate is intended to ensure that funds for mission are provided on an annual basis, with additional return to cover administrative costs and any rise in inflation. In that way, the endowment payout remains a component of the nonprofit's annual budget, but the financial strength of the endowment is not diminishing over time.

As you evaluate the efforts of a nonprofit to establish, maintain, and grow an endowment, you might inquire about the cost to operate a specific endowed program. You can use the Form 990 tax return and audited financial statements to verify the legitimacy of such cost projection. With that information, you can calculate the principal necessary to generate an adequate return to fully fund such endowed program. For example, if a program of a nonprofit were to cost $3 million each year to operate, the corpus of the endowment would need to be $100 million to generate a 3 percent return to fund the entire program year after year. When you couple that information with a review of a nonprofit's ability to fundraise, including its planned giving program, you begin to see the trajectory and timeline that a disciplined nonprofit might pursue to achieve a goal of being fully endowed in perpetuity.

Alignment of Endowment Investment and Charitable Mission

For any nonprofit organization that has matured to establish one or more endowments, the fiduciary demands of its board of directors begin to increase significantly. It is a profound responsibility to steward funds that have been restricted for use, exclusively and in perpetuity, for a charitable purpose. Such funds are often the product of a series of lifetime and planned gifts of many philanthropists who share a common vision coming together across generations.

UPMIFA articulates the fiduciary standards of nonprofit boards and leadership when maintaining an endowment. UPMIFA's fiduciary standards were drafted to lean toward the "modern portfolio theory" of investment. Modern portfolio theory is a mathematical framework with the dual objective to achieve maximum return while minimizing risk through a strategy of robust investment diversification. The economist Harry Markowitz first introduced the concept of modern portfolio theory. In his biographical sketch that he submitted in connection with his receipt of the Nobel Prize for this work, he wrote the following:

> The basic concepts of portfolio theory came to me one afternoon in the library while reading John Burr Williams's Theory of Investment Value. Williams proposed that the value of a stock should equal the present value of its future dividends. Since future dividends are uncertain, I interpreted Williams's proposal to be to value a stock by its expected future dividends. But if the investor were only interested in expected values of securities, he or she would only be interested in the expected value of the portfolio; and to maximize the expected value of a portfolio one need

invest only in a single security. This, I knew, was not the way investors did or should act. Investors diversify because they are concerned with risk as well as return. Variance came to mind as a measure of risk. The fact that portfolio variance depended on security covariances added to the plausibility of the approach. Since there were two criteria, risk, and return, it was natural to assume that investors selected from the set of Pareto optimal risk-return combinations.[60]

There is a certain brilliance in Markowitz's analysis and the mathematics he worked out to assess the risk-return trade-off. This work substantiates a compelling need for diversity of investment in any portfolio of endowed assets. For better or worse, this same principle runs through the UPMIFA body of law. Before modern portfolio theory had been widely accepted as the primary method of constructing investment portfolios, the investment of endowments was prone to second-guessing by the legal system. Many considered the use of financial products like puts, calls, and short sales to be overly risky for institutional funds. Underdiversification in "safe" assets like real estate and corporate bonds were a common strategy. The legal uncertainty of what a prudent investor should do led investment managers to adopt investment strategies that were inconsistent with the risk profile of their clients and likely led to lower returns. Once modern portfolio theory had been broadly accepted, it became the basis for the prudent investor standard under UPMIFA.

When examining an endowment, while intergenerational growth of purchasing power is the ideal, it's also important to understand in what areas the endowment is invested. When modern portfolio theory

---

60   Harry M. Markowitz, "Biographical," from *Les Prix Nobel: The Nobel Prizes 1990,* Editor Tore Frängsmyr, [Nobel Foundation], Stockholm, 1991.

exclusively drives investment strategies, there may be outcomes that run contrary to your philanthropic plan. When you don't consider the types of investments that may be permitted in a nonprofit's investment policy statement, the potential exists for a macroeconomic paradox in the achievement of a philanthropist's goals. Under strict modern portfolio theory, the goal is only to maximize return in the markets. This is done without consideration of the mission of the nonprofit organization.

Let's take a $1 million endowment, with an annual 4 percent payout requirement per its spending policy. The annual distribution should be $40,000, which is nice recurring annual support for a charitable program. You can do a lot with $40,000. You can help a lot of people. But consider if the $1 million were invested in for-profit companies with no consideration of the nonprofit's mission. If your nonprofit organization is agnostic to the underlying types of investments as long as it's meeting its return, then that nonprofit runs the risk of doing more harm and creating more of the problems the nonprofit is trying to combat. A for-profit organization that's exploiting a market lead in technology to the detriment of segments of the population might be the one getting the $1 million to continue its activities, while the nonprofit organization is allocating $40,000 to its mission. Now, consider the trillions of dollars of endowments invested in the markets.

When considering a gift to an endowment, you can engage in deeper due diligence to determine whether the nonprofit's investment policies are conscious of this issue and whether limitation, restrictions, or even affirmative guidance on types of investments is documented and memorialized in the organization's IPS.

When you serve on a board and are asked to consider an IPS appropriately related to mission, can you seek those investments that generate outcomes in alignment with your nonprofit's charitable purpose? Is it possible to not only generate $40,000 for programmatic support but to have the $1 million invested in mission-aligned opportunities? The successful achievement of the objectives of both nonprofit organizations and philanthropists is likely dependent on the alignment of mission and investment strategy when managing endowed assets. If a goal of a philanthropist is to restrict pools of funds in ways that eliminate gaps, disparities, and injustices, then you will be looking for nonprofit organizations that are thoughtful in terms of mission and/or program-related investments for their endowment portfolios.

Program-Related and Mission-Related Investments

In terms of investment of endowed assets, a nonprofit organization's use of capital may be seen along a spectrum, with pure program funding/grants at one end and pure financial return on the other. The two end points on the spectrum are generally referred to as "program-related investments" and "mission-related investments."

Program-related investments (PRIs) are a hybrid between grants and investments but still involve the primary purpose of having a charitable impact, e.g., below-market-rate loans, loan guarantees, and certain equity investments with a below-market rate of return. The IRS promulgated rules for private foundations related to PRIs.[61] No such rules have been established for public charities.

In the Form 990 tax return of a nonprofit, found in schedule D, part VIII, the IRS requires private foundations to report "Investments—Program Related" and offers guidance in the instructions that explains as follows: "[p]rogram related investments are investments made primarily to accomplish the organization's exempt purposes

---

61   See Internal Revenue Code §4944.

rather than to produce income. Common examples of program-related investments include student loans and notes receivable from other exempt organizations that obtained the funds to pursue the filing organization's exempt function."

Public charities are not subject to requirements as stringent as private foundations. Public charities are permitted, under the law, to expand their activities from PRIs to include broader mission-related investments within their investment policy statement.

Mission-related investments (MRIs) are market-based investments that complement a public charity's overall mission. MRIs can take many forms, such as deposits in community development banks, loans, or equity investments directly in companies or in intermediaries (like funds or partnerships) that seek to advance one or more social aims. A nonprofit dedicated to environmental causes may seek to invest in publicly traded manufacturers of electric vehicles, clean-energy generators, or recycling technologies. A religious organization may require no investment in companies that manufacture or sell alcohol. There are many such examples.

You might also describe many MRIs as forms of "social impact investing" or "venture philanthropy." Impact investments and venture philanthropy take more into account than simply risk and return. As an economic matter, impact investments are often financial products that capture and commoditize goodwill, an economic attribute that modern portfolio theory generally ignores.

In contrast to PRIs, the IRS provides no real guidance regarding any definition of an MRI. UPMIFA, however, establishes a list of factors for consideration when making investment decisions, which includes a factor on which MRIs may be based. A fiduciary of institutional and endowed funds is instructed under UPMIFA that, to fulfill one's responsibilities and duties to the nonprofit, the fiduciary shall consider the following factors when contemplating an investment:

General economic conditions

- Effects of inflation and deflation

- Tax consequences

- Role of each investment in the overall portfolio

- Expected total return from income and appreciation

- The charity's other resources

- An asset's special relationship or value to the institution's charitable purpose

While investors following the prudent investor rule may default to modern portfolio theory, UPMIFA does provide grounds for a nonprofit organization to consider an asset's special relationship or value to the institution's charitable purpose. Under this current legal framework, the decision of a nonprofit to deploy endowed assets to effect a PRI and MRI strategy will always rely heavily on this UPMIFA investment factor.

Harkening back to the perspective that an investment policy statement is the output of significant organizational learning and institutional knowledge, you can see this reflected in the maturation of a nonprofit as it begins to explore endowments. An IPS is an inevitable requirement to maintain an endowment. It's an extremely difficult exercise for a nonprofit and its board to invest institutional funds while pursuing PRIs and MRIs, managing risk, and trying to increase purchasing power from one generation to the next. It's one thing to imbue an IPS with restrictions and guidance regarding risk tolerance, but it's an entirely different affair to craft a mission-focused IPS. By its nature, such an IPS will need to describe, affirmatively, types of investments that correlate to mission and programmatic activities. This will likely be an ever-evolving process based on experience. It is a classic example of why a nonprofit must be equipped with advanced skills in organizational learning and institutional knowledge retention to be mature enough to establish and maintain one or more endowments.

There are additional questions the board of the nonprofit and its investment managers should consider regarding its charitable mission in relation to its IPS:

- How much of the overall portfolio/assets of the charitable organization should be dedicated to MRIs or PRIs?

- What are the risks associated with the facts and circumstances of an MRI or PRI in relation to the return expectations of the portfolio/assets of the charitable organization?

- How liquid is the MRI or the PRI? Is there an exit strategy? Are there restrictions on transfer?

- Should all MRI or PRI activity be housed in a subsidiary of the charitable organization to separate liabilities arising out of the investment from the corporate entity that manages its other charitable programs?

- Are MRIs or PRIs permitted in the charitable organization's articles, constitution, and bylaws? If not, is a change warranted?

These are all prudent questions that reflect organizational learning. The by-product of these questions should be an ever-advancing IPS, acting as the living embodiment of institutional knowledge.

The Democratization of the Endowment

When you understand the mechanics and operation of an endowment, you can also see that historically they've been the tools of the rich to hold assets in private foundations used in connection with their personal philanthropy. Fred Goff's invention of the Cleveland Foundation democratized the endowment. That's its brilliance. With the advent of the community foundation, endowments became accessible to everyone. Over the last century, public charities of all types and in all sectors began to establish endowments. In the hundred years since the founding of the Cleveland Foundation, we now see hundreds of thousands of endowments available for any philanthropist to incorporate into a philanthropic plan. This isn't just in other community foundations. This trend runs across the entire field of public charities in the United States—hospitals, universities, museums, symphonies, gardens, orphanages, food kitchens, free medical clinics, and homeless shelters all have endowments today. Historically speaking, from the first human to the modern-day United States, this approach to philanthropy, through organized endowments held by public charities, has never existed before on this planet. But it exists today. And it's an essential part of the fabric of the United States economy.

Not only did Fred Goff democratize the endowment, but he also set a new standard for governance of a public charity. The board of the Cleveland Foundation exemplifies modern nonprofit governance, geared to support organizational learning and the memorialization of institutional knowledge. Fred's vision of self-perpetuating boards of directors, serving without pay, for limited terms of service, is now seen throughout the US nonprofit sector.

Philanthropy has come a long way since ancient Greece. The grand American experiment has resulted in a robust landscape of public charities, community foundations, and endowments. We're at the dawn of an impressive era of philanthropy as the transition of generational wealth from the baby boomers begins. This marks a period of hypergrowth in intergenerational equity for the nonprofits that are ready. For the philanthropist, if you're going to fulfill your philanthropic plan, your job is to identify those nonprofits that are ready or help the ones you love to be ready.

PART 4

Your Philanthropic Plan

To give away money is an easy matter and in any man's power. But to decide to whom to give it, and how large, and when, and for what purpose and how, is neither in every man's power nor an easy matter.

—ARISTOTLE

CHAPTER 15

The Beaufort Fund

Driving south from my hometown of Charleston on Highway 17 takes you through the Lowcountry of South Carolina, through four counties—Beaufort, Colleton, Hampton, and Jasper—until you finally reach Savannah at the border with Georgia. For much of the way, it's a two-lane country highway that travels through miles of live oaks. Sometimes the trees reach out over the road, making it feel like you are driving through a green tunnel. But every now and again, you come out of the tunnel to a great expanse where the road draws a thin line over the marsh flats. In every direction you look, you see marsh grass stretching out to touch the horizon, dotted by the occasional island hummock in the distance. Then suddenly you pass through periods of cypress swamps and over rivers, past an occasional country store and boiled-peanut or basket-weaver stand. History stands still in this part of South Carolina—or rather, history always feels present to me when I drive through this area. It's also a place of mysteries waiting to be solved, hidden in the shadows of oak trees, draped in Spanish moss, amid the rust and ruins of an old South that continues to touch the present.

Beaufort County covers almost all the coast except for a sliver of Colleton County to the north where the Combahee River reaches to the ocean. A sign marks the county line between Colleton and Beaufort, indicating where Harriet Tubman of Underground Railroad fame helped Union soldiers defeat a Confederate regiment. Hampton and Jasper Counties are inland, just to the west of Highway 17.

Beaufort is the largest town of the area. Barrier islands run down the remaining coast of South Carolina. Many of these islands contain resorts or gated communities. Harbor, Dataw, and Fripp Islands are all known for their golf courses, beautiful scenery, and more deer than you can possibly imagine. Hilton Head lies just south of Beaufort and may be one of the more famous resort islands of this coast. Nearby is Parris Island, where US Marines have trained since 1915.

You'll also pass other islands that have retained more of their Gullah Geechee history. St. Helena and Daufuskie Islands remain largely owned by African Americans. In these islands and many parts of Colleton, Jasper, and Hampton Counties, a good amount of the real estate is heirs' property. Heirs' property is land that is jointly owned by the descendants of a deceased person whose estate did not clear probate. The person died without a will. If you don't have a will, the state's laws of intestacy dictate the division of property among certain living descendants. If multiple generations die without making a will, the ownership of the property will become fractured. It's not unusual to have heirs' property with divided interests in the hundreds. The descendants, or heirs, have the right to use the property, but they don't have a clear or marketable title. This ownership issue tanks the value of the property and creates exposures for unscrupulous real estate developers to take advantage.

Driving through these four counties, you see a juxtaposition of wealthy communities against poor rural communities, often vestiges of slave times and the aftermath of the rice plantation communities of prior centuries. This is rural South Carolina, fraught with the same problems you see all over the rural South. There is almost no widespread broadband access to the internet. Telemedicine and online educational degrees aren't accessible. All the benefits of living in a "remote" but connected world do not exist here. It's just remote. If you were to look up this area in the "Opportunity Atlas" developed by Raj Chetty, where tax information is used to track upward mobility and opportunity in different places across the United States since the mid-1800s, you would see that this area is a study in contrast: a lot of red signifying limited to no opportunity next to small pockets of blue and green representing affluence. It has been this way for generations. Today, the populations of Hampton, Colleton, and Jasper Counties largely work in the resorts, gated communities, and service jobs in the wealthier Beaufort County.

One of the mysteries that comes from this place, at least in my nonprofit world, is the Beaufort Fund. The Beaufort Fund is an example of philanthropy that seeks to address challenges of access to basic needs and opportunities in these four counties. The fund grew up from the area itself. Formed in 1998, the Beaufort Fund was established as a "field of interest" fund at the Coastal Community Foundation of South Carolina through a significant gift that included certain directions of the donor. Much like the Cleveland Foundation, which has a specific geographic service area, the Beaufort Fund was established to make grants to nonprofits that provided services only in the counties of Beaufort, Colleton, Hampton, and Jasper, South Carolina.

Since its inception, the Beaufort Fund has awarded more than $11 million in total to over two hundred nonprofit organizations. More recently, in 2023 the Beaufort Fund awarded $1.4 million in grant funding to 117 organizations. Grants are offered at three levels: Genesis Grants of $10,000, First-Time Grants of $15,000, and Operational Grants of $25,000. What is interesting is that, for the most part, these grants are for general operating support.

To my knowledge, this is the largest endowment with an active grant-making program that has ever been created in South Carolina. What immediately caught my attention when I first heard about this fund? The original donor requested to be anonymous until death. I have never seen the "anonymous donor" designation attributed to a fund of this size in South Carolina.

I also think the Beaufort Fund is a notable example of a partnership between a philanthropist and a nonprofit, the output of which is impressive. For more than a quarter century, the Coastal Community Foundation of South Carolina, or CCF, has been the champion of this fund.

The origin of the Coastal Community Foundation goes back to a meeting of Louis Fischer and Paul Harris at a Shriners convention in Chicago in 1919. Fischer would return to Charleston to connect with his friend and World War I veteran T. Wilbur "Buddy" Thornhill. Together, in 1920 they founded the first Rotary in my hometown, known today as the Rotary Club of Charleston. My town's Rotary was prolific in its creation of other clubs and nonprofits in the area, including the Coastal Community Foundation in 1974, with an initial gift of $9,000.

I enjoy the thought that, in my hometown, a chapter of Paul Harris's Rotary launched Fred Goff's prototype community foundation. As of 2024, the fiftieth anniversary of the founding of the Coastal Community Foundation, the model has proven highly successful. In 2023, the Coastal Community Foundation reported total assets of $491 million, held across 838 funds, with a staff of thirty-eight. The Coastal Community Foundation awarded $30 million in grants and scholarships that year alone. Ten years ago, CCF held assets worth almost $200 million. That's an increase of 150 percent in net worth of CCF in just a decade. It would not surprise me if ten years from now CCF would be managing and holding over $1 billion in total assets.

For more than twenty-five years, the Coastal Community Foundation has maintained the Beaufort Fund, and until recently, the foundation kept secret the identity of the philanthropists who established this fund. Since 1998, there have been four CEOs at the Coastal Community Foundation as well as numerous turnovers of board members and staff. No one broke the promise of anonymity.

I represent many of the organizations that were grantees of the Beaufort Fund. I can tell you that no one knew. The identity of the donor was a secret. The Coastal Community Foundation holds a luncheon every year for this fund. It's a great chance to honor the grantees. A lot of people attend. Still, no one in the general public, including the grantees, knew who made the lead gift and who conceptualized this fund, or even that they were in attendance for all those lunches.

In April 2022, the Coastal Community Foundation revealed the donors to be Alan and Joanne Moses.

Alan Moses died at age eighty-seven in 2018, and Joanne Moses passed away at eighty-nine in 2021.

They gave their permission that, following their death, the Coastal Community Foundation might reveal their identity.

"Alan and Joanne Moses could go down in South Carolina history as some of the most generous philanthropists our state has ever seen, and yet, they were the last people who would have sought such a distinction," said Darrin Goss, president and CEO of the Coastal

Community Foundation. "In so many ways they embodied the best of what philanthropy stands for."[62]

Joanne grew up in Chevy Chase, Maryland, and attended Duke University in North Carolina. Joanne's father passed away unexpectedly of a heart attack when she was eleven. Alan was also familiar with adversity at a young age. Alan's father had a series of strokes when Alan was still in high school. These strokes affected his father's abilities. Alan grew up in New Jersey and later went to Trinity College in Connecticut for his undergraduate degree. Both Joanne and Alan made it through school on full scholarships. The transition to college and adulthood could have been very difficult considering the adversity they'd both faced early in life, but they were surrounded by good people, and many opportunities were provided to them. The awareness of how lucky they were, coupled with values rooted in fairness and justice, may have compelled the couple in the long run to create the Beaufort Fund and to support so many other charitable endeavors.

After college, Alan and Joanne each moved to New York City. They met at a party in the city and were married pretty soon after. They had two children, Bill and Anne, and settled in Chatham, New Jersey. Chatham would be their home for the next thirty years.

Joanne was a homemaker, but she stayed active in many community activities and responsibilities, even volunteering for their local EMS. Friends describe her as outgoing and an avid, competitive golfer. In the early years of their marriage, Alan would complete his MBA at New York University and take a job with an investment firm

---

62 Quoted in Abigail Darlington, "Late Anonymous Donors Who Created and Gave Millions through The Beaufort Fund Revealed to Be 'Unassuming' Dataw Island Couple," Coastal Community Foundation, April 6, 2022, https://coastalcommunityfoundation.org/late-anonymous-donors-who-created-and-gave-millions-through-the-beaufort-fund-revealed-to-be-unassuming-dataw-island-couple/#:~:text="Alan%20and%20Joanne%20Moses%20could,of%20what%20philanthropy%20stands%20for.

on Water Street in lower Manhattan. As he advanced in his career, Alan would be one of the pioneers of the "leveraged buyout." Most notably, he worked to help his employer, Dominick & Dominick, acquire the furniture manufacturer Drexel Heritage. Instead of taking Drexel apart and selling its assets for more value the way it often happens with leveraged buyouts, Alan's firm invested in the operations of Drexel and increased retail sales drastically.[63] His story reminds me of Herbert Taylor's turnaround of Aluminum Company that inspired the Four-Way Test for Rotaries worldwide.

Alan worked in a period of American economics where our country's focus was to grow value in the long term. Alan invested in this future, based on his beliefs in long-term principles. He was sowing seeds for a level of wealth that even he didn't imagine at the time.

While they raised their family in New Jersey, Joanne's heart was in the South. The couple always said they would retire there. In 1988, on a vacation to Beaufort, South Carolina, they came back home with a purchase agreement on a lot on Dataw Island, a gated community just outside the town of Beaufort. Alan told his employer that once their house was built, they would retire. A year later, he and Joanne did just that.

Much of their wealth accumulated after they moved to Dataw Island. That was during a time in their lives when they were already set for retirement.

The subsequent jumps in wealth didn't change who they were as people. They didn't dress or act any differently. Half the furniture in their house was handmade by Alan. Joanne was known to serve peanuts in a crystal bowl that she'd won in a golf tournament. While

---

63   Shane Williams, "Drexel Furniture Company," North Carolina History Project, accessed June 3, 2024, https://northcarolinahistory.org/encyclopedia/drexel-furniture-company/.

the commemorative bowl might have been intended for display, all form had to have a function. According to their family, they thought of themselves as ordinary people who'd gotten incredibly lucky over the years. At their core, Alan and Joanne were "very down to earth, just plain folks," according to Bill Moses, their son. While Alan was successful in his career, it was only later in life that the couple saw major returns on their investments.

"My father ended up making some very good investments," Bill Moses said, "but they always saw themselves as ordinary people who had gotten lucky and could just as easily have gotten unlucky."[64]

"They were very cognizant of the fact that they lived the life they did as adults due to the generosity of others, and they felt it was their duty to create such opportunities for those coming behind them," said their daughter, Anne McCaffrey.[65] Notwithstanding the challenges that Alan and Joanne faced during their childhoods, they grew up with strong community values and work ethic. Their scholarships to college left a lasting impact on them. That was an amazing economic benefit that put them on the path to success. These experiences instilled in them a desire to give back, to share their opportunities and success with those who followed, and to give others a similar leg up.

My local newspaper, the *Post & Courier*, wrote this to describe the Moseses after the passing of Joanne:

> People who work with philanthropists say no two are alike. A donor might put a family name on a fund to cultivate a culture of giving in future generations. Or, a donor might name a scholarship after someone who has died. Donors can also use their own names as a way to generate more support for a cause. A lot of giving happens because of who

---

64   Quoted in Darlington, "Late Anonymous Donors."

65   Quoted in Darlington, "Late Anonymous Donors."

is making the ask—a high-profile donor can ask other high-profile donors to give.

But Alan and Joanne Moses did not fit into any of those categories. They perceived themselves to be ordinary people who made some lucky investments. Giving anonymously allowed them to live and act as they really were, rather than play a role.[66]

I never met Alan or Joanne, but I'd like to think that our paths might have crossed at a Coastal Community Foundation event or a celebration of one of my many nonprofit clients that I now realize they funded. I know I worked on projects they financially supported. I bear witness to the good they placed in this world. Before 2022, I had no actual knowledge of them.

In some ways, Alan and Joanne also remind me of Fred and Frances Goff, the founders of the Cleveland Foundation. They came from humble means. Both couples spent considerable time thinking, together, about their communities and how they could make them better. While Fred and Frances might have created a vehicle in the form of the *community foundation*, whereby anyone in the community may engage as a philanthropist, Alan and Joanne are the best examples of philanthropists, almost a century later, using a community foundation to its maximum potential.

I feel like Alan and Joanne were the types of people who, when they bear witness to such contrasts as they could see in these four

---

66   Kelly Jean Kelly, "The Millionaires Next Door: Dataw Couple Anonymously Gave Millions to Beaufort Area," *The Post and Courier*, June 8, 2022, https://www.postand-courier.com/hilton-head/the-millionaires-next-door-dataw-couple-anonymously-gave-millions-to-beaufort-area/article_83b56dea-cfc9-11ec-b38a-13d286516b80.html#:~:text=Mackenzie%20Scott%20donates%20%242.5M%20to%20South%20Carolina%20education%20nonprofit&text=But%20Alan%20and%20Joanne%20Moses,rather%20than%20play%20a%20role.

South Carolina counties, would respond not with guilt but with a sense of community responsibility. *What can I do to help?* "After they retired and moved down to Beaufort, they really loved the area, but they also saw a lot of people who needed help," Bill said.[67] I've met many couples who retire to this part of South Carolina, and I appreciate the new perspective they bring to these communities. They have a neutrality to this place that enables them to connect and to see new ways they can help and, in doing so, make this place home.

The Moseses' Philanthropic Plan

The start of any philanthropic plan is a vision. Alan and Joanne Moses envisioned a fully funded endowment at the Coastal Community Foundation. The fund would be restricted to support nonprofits providing service in the four named South Carolina counties. An award committee would be part of the fund, and it would advise the foundation where it would like distributions of funds to go. The committee would be made up of residents of the four counties. Basic needs, like healthcare and education, were to take priority. The fund would not be permitted to make distributions of support to capital campaigns and animal welfare projects. This was the blueprint of the Beaufort Fund.

I have heard from several people with CCF that the Moseses had two additional rules that accompanied the Beaufort Fund: (1) no one could ever disclose that they had started the Beaufort Fund until after they both died, and (2) no one could ever disclose how much they'd contributed, ever.

Early in their plan, they fully funded the Beaufort Fund as a permanently endowed field-of-interest fund with a permanently

---

67   Quoted in Darlington, "Late Anonymous Donors."

restricted corpus. Once the Beaufort Fund was fully funded, Alan and Joanne immediately shifted their donative strategy. No longer did they make gifts of restricted corpus. They embraced an urgency of now in their giving. All their gifts thereafter would be currently expendable. While this handbook often conceptualizes that your planned gift will go to an endowment, the Moseses made endowment giving the first priority. Once the endowment was fully funded, the Moseses shifted to current needs. They even made the charitable gifts in their estate planning to be currently expendable. This sequence of giving reflects philanthropists who prioritized saving adequately for the future first, then shifting all energy and funds toward immediate needs.

Secret Millionaires Next Door

Anonymity was a critical component to the Moseses' deployment of their philanthropic plan. It was their primary tool, and in its own way, it was a statement. They might have decided, together, that their giving must be devoid of ego. As if it might take away from the mission if their presence were felt. They might have thought that if they didn't imprint their ego on this fund, it would potentially feel more accessible for others to donate to or participate in.

Anonymity was also a burden to them. Alan passed away twenty years after the fund was established; for Joanne, it was twenty-three years after. That's a long time to keep a big secret in a small community. Neighbors and friends would ask them point blank if they were responsible for various charitable undertakings. They were unrelenting in their denial. How could you tell one friend but not another? Once the cat was out of the bag, there would be no stopping the word of mouth. It bothered them, but to expand the secret would undermine the plan.

It's also important to note that they included their children, Bill and Anne, in the circle of trust as additional partners in their philanthropic plan. According to Bill, their parents made it clear to him and his sister that they were giving their wealth to charity, primarily the Beaufort Fund. When parents include children, they recognize that the children and grandchildren, really the entire descending family, is participating in the philanthropic plan. I've seen it go the other way, with parents who did not tell their children. I've been in those battles where heirs object to the charitable gift. It's unfortunate on many levels.

Award Committee

One of the details I really like about Alan and Joanne is that they served on the Beaufort Fund's grant-making committee that reviewed applications and made award recommendations. It was the offering of this committee structure, coupled with the ongoing administrative and logistic support of the Coastal Community Foundation, that drew the Moseses to establish the Beaufort Fund at the Coastal Community Foundation.

For the rest of their lifetimes, they served on this committee. Alan and Joanne did the same work as fellow committee members. They participated in site visits where they got a close view of different nonprofits' needs. Alan brought the financial thoughtfulness of his investment career to their work, while Joanne was the extravert who connected with people and often did the talking. Foundation staff members have told me about times when the consensus of the committee might have been different from either Alan's or Joanne's perspective. While they would speak their mind, in the end Alan and Joanne always agreed with the consensus. For those few staff members who knew their secret, they were impressed at those occasional moments.

Since no one knew that the Moseses were the source of the Beaufort Fund, people opened up to them. They appeared to be volunteers on a committee. I think this was really important to them—that they could seek out the truth of the needs of their community. To me, this reflects a grounding in the ethics of truth and information. By diminishing their ego, not pulling rank in the award committee, or being the "founders," they were able to engage with people authentically. From the nonprofit leaders with whom they developed long-term relationships, they learned that a nonprofit's real needs were to keep the lights on and meet payroll. They realized that the administrative costs, like staff salary, all really went to mission. These individuals worked hard for mission. Without them, neither a nonprofit nor a mission would exist. The closeness they maintained with the grantees over time created trust.

Trust Philanthropy

The ability of an endowment to distribute funds for general operating support of a nonprofit grantee is a key transitional thought to philanthropy in the twenty-first century. Alan and Joanne were the pioneers of this growing style of *trust* philanthropy. But there are others whose philanthropy is following this trend—like Chuck Feeney, who secretly gave away $8 billion before his death in 2023, and MacKenzie Scott, who gave away $640 million in 2024 to more than 360 organizations, allowing them to use the funds as they thought best.

> Find the people doing the good work, fund them, and get out of the way.

As baby boomers design their own generational transfer of wealth, a possible future of philanthropy may hold increased emphasis on evaluation of nonprofits to identify the ones that may be trusted with unrestricted gifts of support. Find the people doing the good work, fund them, and get out of the way. The Moseses' philanthropic plan makes a lot of practical sense.

Paul Harris and Rotary spoke to community responsibility and fellowship. Fred Goff and the community foundation democratized the endowment to be accessible to anyone.

Philanthropists like Alan and Joanne Moses uphold a new standard whereby philanthropy can be focused on trust of the nonprofit organization based on authentic engagement.

The key to trust philanthropy is for donors and nonprofits to get to know one another and for the donor to see that the nonprofit has strong internal controls married with effective leadership based on cultivation and attraction of talent through thoughtful succession planning. Because no one knew that Alan and Joanne were the funders, they took down barriers and biases that might have otherwise existed, and the Moseses were able to connect with people in their home community.

I define philanthropy as the output of philanthropists and nonprofits working together collaboratively. The collaboration of Alan and Joanne Moses with the Coastal Community Foundation exemplifies this definition, the output of which is the Beaufort Fund.

As I think about the philanthropic plan of Alan and Joanne Moses, it's clear to me that the impact of the Beaufort Fund will continue for the foreseeable future. Alan and Joanne have shown us that nonprofits like the Coastal Community Foundation are our champions that carry forward a shared mission after we pass from this world. This is the type of trust that recognizes that after you die, the nonprofit will be solely responsible for the endowment. Giving future leaders of the nonprofit the most flexibility regarding decisions while keeping the corpus restricted from expenditure is an ideal arrangement. I'd hope

Fred Goff might agree if he were alive today. This trust extends to the grantees of the Beaufort Fund, who are given the freedom and liberty to deploy grants in the manner that the organization, and not the philanthropist, deems appropriate.

I also think at some deeper level that Alan and Joanne are telling us, "You just might not know who out there is a philanthropist." It's like the old movie plot line of the super wealthy individual pretending to be a regular person in disguise in order to identify worthy individuals to help. It's an equally important message today—treat everyone well. You never know who might be the secret millionaires next door. There's a message of hope in that thought too. Secret angels are real. There is a charitable side to all of us, and if you can harness that side, you can become a philanthropist, with a message and a mission to be expressed in your own philanthropy.

I've been lucky to work on many projects that I now realize the Moseses funded, and I've had a chance to learn about them from their family and friends. I've been wondering what Alan and Joanne might think about this chapter. My gut says that they would tell me I've made a mistake. Their philanthropy was not about them, no matter how much we might want to celebrate them and their example. Their philanthropy was about these four counties, this corner of South Carolina. It was about the two-hundred-plus nonprofits that have received grants in the last quarter century. It is about the community that the Beaufort Fund itself lifts up and celebrates. It is a love letter from Alan and Joanne to their home. I think that is the true vision of their philanthropic plan.

CHAPTER 16

Envisioning Your Philanthropic Plan

I n this handbook, we have explored the role of the philanthropist in society. We have examined three disciplines of philanthropy. We have considered meditations to amplify empathy and foresight. We have considered ways in which you may evaluate a nonprofit organization through the ethics of information and truth. We have also looked at how you can help the leaders of a nonprofit engage in organizational learning and memorialization of institutional knowledge, which are the twin characteristics of a successful nonprofit. At this time, however, we've reached the point where we need to consider your philanthropic plan.

If we define a philanthropist as an individual who has a capacity of empathy to not only express charitable actions but to do so with foresight pursuant to a plan to maximize impact, how do we define a *philanthropic plan*?

A philanthropic plan is a timeline and strategy of gifts and bequests of wealth, often culminating in a planned gift, to your nonprofit champions.

There are five aspects to the creation of a philanthropic plan that are common for most philanthropists:

1. Conceiving a vision of your philanthropy, which includes identifying your nonprofit partner(s)

2. Forming a philanthropic team to help you create and memorialize your philanthropic plan

3. Identifying the assets you will contribute and the strategy you will use to fund your philanthropic plan

4. Drafting an agreement or legal instrument to memorialize and effect your philanthropic plan

5. Crafting your message for the future

Identifying the professionals to help you, identifying the assets you desire to donate, and memorializing your gift into a legal document represent the nuts and bolts of your philanthropic plan. But it's the calling of your vision to you and then connecting to the nonprofit with which you wish to partner in mission—that is the personal part.

When you're thinking about a planned gift, you're also thinking about death. In the context of a planned gift, death is more of a reflection upon this question: "What was my mission in life?" It's not often we pause and ask ourselves, not why we exist, but instead what our mission is. We get to decide our mission. Our individual mission speaks our truth. If you reach this place in your philanthropic musings, many people think about what they want to tell those who follow, their children, family, or future generations. For your philanthropic plan to have a positive impact on your life, as you read this part 4, think about your mission in life and your message to the future.

Identifying the Nonprofits That Share Your Mission

The first step is the hardest. That is true for so many things in life, including creating your philanthropic plan.

First, you must identify the object of your affection. An object of your affection is a charitable organization on which you will focus energy and wealth, ultimately leading to a planned gift upon your death.

The "object of your affection" is the way our court system refers to your heirs in your will. It's a strange phrase with a familial connotation, but it's apt for a planned gift to a nonprofit organization.

To what cause will you be called?

Most philanthropists draw from their personal experience when considering the positive effect they want to have on society. Philanthropists may be wrestling with traumas in life that they have personally experienced. They may have lost a loved one, a parent, or a child. In other cases, philanthropists may have borne witness to some powerful event and, as empathic beings, hear a call to action. Others may wish to give back to institutions or nonprofits that gave them so much.

Alan and Joanne Moses felt compelled to *pay it forward* in return for the opportunities they were afforded in life. They wanted to help their home community in a broad manner. They found their nonprofit partner in the Coastal Community Foundation. They were attracted to the Coastal Community Foundation due to its people, structure, and maturity. The foundation would be able to process grants across the four counties, with an award committee composed of local residents, responding to the needs of the region. This structure would continue after they die.

For some people, a philanthropic calling will be readily apparent, like the attraction of the Moseses to the Coastal Community Foundation in order to help their home community. But that's not always the case. The idea of philanthropy can easily overwhelm you. You play a part in democratic capitalism, not just of today's world but in the continuum of human history. With philanthropy, we aim to improve the lives of future generations of our species.

These are big thoughts. But sometimes you have to start small. As we learned in part 2, you can unlock the Helper's High by recalling moments when others have helped you and you have helped others. If you write down these experiences and maintain the two lists of generosity, given and received, you will begin to call your plan to you. Keep these two generosity lists. Add to them as events occur or you recall forgotten experiences. Consider any patterns that you see. Consider how different experiences make you feel. Over time, go back and read your entries. Look for common words or recurring ideas or images. If you write for long enough, themes will emerge. Themes give rise to insights. Insights can provide direction. Use the other visualization exercises in part 2 to open yourself to a philanthropic calling. As you think on these experiences, try to write an expression of your charitable mission. Over time, try to distill those thoughts into a mission statement. Let that mission statement guide you to organizations that share a similar purpose.

If you use part 2 to help you find your philanthropic mission, part 3 will enable you to seek out those nonprofits that operate within your philanthropic interests. Part 3 contains subjective and objective measures you might use to compare nonprofits to each other. The beneficiary of your philanthropic plan should be an organization that excels in organizational learning and retention of institutional knowledge or an organization that you desire to help pursue such skills.

This is the process to identify the object of your affection—your nonprofit champion.

CHAPTER 17

Your Philanthropic Team

I t is possible that you may develop and deploy a philanthropic plan without any help, but more often than not, given the complexity of the modern world, particularly as it relates to the transfer of legal title to assets, you will need a team of professionals to assist you. Your philanthropic team may include some or all of the following roles:

- Development officer

- Attorney

- Financial planner

- Certified public accountant (CPA)

- Family members

This chapter describes the types of relationships you may have with each of these professionals. It's possible that any one of the foregoing may be able to provide the skills of others. A complete team doesn't always mean that all these professionals are represented. For example, a good CPA, working with a tax attorney, may displace the need for a financial planner. This is normal. What's important is that you trust your team and that they're committed to your philanthropic mission.

Your ability to coordinate these professionals and their openness to work with one another is important to ensure a holistic approach to your philanthropic plan. If you're not the quarterback, you should identify one individual on your team to take the lead, help coordinate efforts, facilitate communication, and ensure that all aspects of your financial and philanthropic goals are addressed.

Lastly, you'll find that some professional roles are well suited to serve as part of your team of "no." If a nonprofit presents a request for funding to you that you are not inclined to support, your team of "no" are the individuals who can decline opportunities on your behalf. Your team can help you establish boundaries around your philanthropy and protect your empathy. However, you should also be mindful when any of them are overzealous and not reflecting your charitable intent.

The Development Officer

Within the nonprofit world, the development or gift officer is the unsung hero. The development officer is not on the team of "no" but instead is always looking for a "yes." The job of the development officer is to cultivate your interest to be a donor of their employer, a nonprofit organization. They work with you first to become an annual donor, then inquire about your interest in a periodic major gift, and then, at the appropriate moment, might ask if you are interested in a planned gift. This work requires high attentiveness to donors. When two or more development officers visit with you at once, you should know that the community is at your door.

Here are some key aspects of a donor's relationship with a development officer:

- **Building trust**: Development officers will work to build trust with you. To do so, they must demonstrate to you their organization's impact and how it maintains accountability. This involves sharing success stories and soliciting your feedback on the organization's programs and activities. Transparency must exist in all communications. This includes giving you real inside views and making honest inquiries into your thoughts. These conversations should not be one sided and littered with rosy assessments or grandiose vision statements.

- **Developing customized philanthropic plans**: Development officers will assist you to identify specific programs or projects in which you might have interest. With any gift proposal, they should outline the impact your gift will have on the organization's mission. Seek data and metrics from your development officer. Integrate that information into your plan, and use it to assess organizational performance over time.

- **Providing recognition and stewardship**: Development officers will work to ensure that you feel appreciated and valued for your contributions to their organization. This involves providing personalized recognition and stewardship, such as thank-you letters, donor events, and other forms of engagement.

Your relationship with any development officer should be collaborative, focused on advancing the organization's mission and creating a positive impact in the community. A good development officer is recording notes from encounters with you into the nonprofit's client relationship management system. These notes are a firsthand record of your donative intent and can serve as guidance to future staff and leaders of the organization.

The relationship of the Coastal Community Foundation and the Moseses is a great example of a partnership supported and driven by development officers. The staff of the Coastal Community Foundation maintain the day-to-day operations of the Beaufort Fund, including closely working with the grant committee, supporting its logistical operation, and managing the investment and distribution of funds. Those staff members who knew kept the Moseses' secret. The years of working together in this manner built trust.

The Attorney

The attorney is the individual who writes your philanthropic plan. The attorney is your scribe. But unlike a court stenographer, the attorney is also your fiduciary. Your attorney owes you several duties. Attorneys play a crucial role in assisting donors with the transfer of funds and assets to one or more organizations to fund your philanthropic plan.

- **Your fiduciary**: As your fiduciary, your attorney may not represent anyone who is adverse to your interests without your consent. Your attorney is required to tell you about these types of conflict in your interests. Your attorney must keep all your communications privileged and confidential. No other person on your team is legally required to maintain confidentiality at the level of your attorney. However, when you open your attorney's communications to others, including any other person on your philanthropic team, those communications may lose the privilege of confidentiality. Be mindful with communications from legal counsel.

- **Drafting legal documents**: Attorneys are responsible for drafting and preparing the necessary legal documents to establish and implement many planned gifts. These include wills, trusts, gift agreements, and other legal instruments. Attorneys ensure that these documents reflect your intentions, comply with legal requirements, and bring your gift to completion. For example, all states have requirements regarding the witnessing of a will's execution. If these are not strictly followed, the will may not be enforceable.

- **Charitable planning techniques**: Attorneys can advise you on various charitable planning techniques to enhance the impact of your gifts. This may include strategies like establishing donor-advised funds, charitable trusts, or a private foundation. Attorneys help you understand the advantages and limitations of each technique and determine the most suitable approach based on your goals and circumstances.

- **Nonprofit due diligence**: Attorneys can assist you in conducting due diligence on nonprofit organizations you wish to support through your philanthropic plan. This may involve reviewing the organization's legal status, governance structure, charitable mission, and overall reputation. Attorneys can also help you make informed decisions and choose reputable organizations that align with your philanthropic goals.

The Financial Planner

A financial planner provides guidance, expertise, and comprehensive financial planning services in connection with your philanthropic plan. A financial planner will review your financial situation, including your assets, income, and liabilities. This assessment helps determine your capacity to make a charitable gift without adversely affecting your personal financial goals and obligations.

I've always thought a key milestone for many philanthropists is when they reach a point when they are financially secure for the rest of their life, like the Moseses when they moved to Dataw Island. I think of this as the *survival* milestone. Once the remainder of your lifetime basic needs are met, how you use the excess reflects whether you are a philanthropist. Your financial planner has the skill set to help you understand what the survival milestone means for you. A financial planner can guide you regarding the resources necessary to meet all your projected lifetime needs and determine, for you, what is excess.

A good financial planner will develop a financial plan that incorporates your philanthropic goals into your personal financial strategy, accounting for your risk tolerance, cash flow needs, and estate-planning objectives. This includes exploring your motivations for making a gift to charity and identifying preferred causes or nonprofits to support. Once you establish your philanthropic plan, a financial planner can provide ongoing monitoring services in connection with your personal financial situation.

The Certified Public Accountant

A CPA can provide financial expertise and guidance in connection with your personal situation and has valuable skills as a preparer of tax returns. A good CPA is like the Swiss Army knife of your philanthropic team. CPAs are often able to step in and fill skills of other team members, including attorneys and financial planners.

- **Tax planning and optimization**: CPAs can analyze the tax implications of different giving strategies and help you to optimize tax benefits. As a member of the team, CPAs tend to have a deeper understanding of tax laws and regulations as they relate to your personal situation. CPAs can provide insights into income tax deductions, estate tax considerations, and capital gains tax implications that might arise in connection with a proposed planned gift.

- **Charitable deduction compliance**: Like attorneys, CPAs can help to ensure that a gift complies with the necessary tax regulations and substantiation requirements for charitable deductions. They help you to understand the documentation needed to claim tax benefits associated with a gift, such as proper acknowledgment letters and appraisals for noncash gifts.

- **Financial analysis and projections**: Like financial planners, CPAs can conduct financial projections to help you understand the financial impact of a gift. They can assess the benefits, risks, and cash flow implications associated with different planned giving options. CPAs can provide insights into how a philanthropic plan may affect your overall financial picture, including retirement planning, investment strategies, and estate planning.

- **Gift valuation and accounting**: CPAs can assist in the valuation of certain in-kind assets involved in gifts, such as real estate, closely held business interests, or complex financial instruments. CPAs can ensure that the valuation is conducted in accordance with relevant accounting standards and tax regulations.

Your Family

While not always considered, members of your family can also play a role in your philanthropic team. They can assist you to assess the nonprofit organizations that are of the most interest to you. If they also hear the call, your family can participate in multigenerational gifts to the same organization. Your family can help to ensure accountability and fulfillment of your planned gift after your death.

In the family setting, you should consider introducing family members to the development officers or other members of your philanthropic team who have been involved in the creation of your philanthropic plan. In most family offices, your family will carry the philanthropic torch of any related private foundation. Teaching your personal representatives and children about your history with your philanthropic beneficiaries, including preserving records of communications and donative intent, can be critical to long-term success in connection with your family's philanthropic mission and identity.

Some people prefer not to include family members on their team or make them aware of their philanthropic plan. This is your decision, based on your life circumstances. But consider the importance of your family when you're gone. You want them not only to support your philanthropic choices but also to refrain from challenging your plan after you die.

This is one of those things that Alan and Joanne Moses did very well. They included their children, Bill and Anne, providing them with advance knowledge of their planning. Bill and Anne have no objection to their parents' philanthropy. They support it. They know that they can participate in the Beaufort Fund if they like, as can their children. They appreciate what their parents have established.

Collectively, the Moseses reflect a family passing the value of the philanthropic way from one generation to the next.

Team Insights

I've been on a few philanthropic teams over the years. From my chair, I don't think there is an ideal configuration of specific roles. The best teams will cover all the skill sets, of course, but what they really do is connect with the philanthropist. My advice to you is to find professionals who relate to you, who will take a real interest in you, and who will translate difficult concepts to your personal situation, making them understandable. I imagine if you're someone reading this book, though, you might already have these roles filled. So what's my advice for you?

- Use your attorney and your CPA on your team of "no." They can protect your empathy, ensure your gift is properly structured, and report any charitable transaction to the IRS.

- You will need a lot of business advice. That is the role of the financial planner. You will need someone to help you define your personal *survival* milestone. Your attorney is not permitted to give you business or nonlegal advice. Your CPA will be focused on tax reporting, auditing, or due diligence. You may be able to do this piece on your own, but a financial planner adds real value more often than not.

- The hardest relationship to manage on your philanthropic team is often that between the development officer and your family. My advice is to be transparent. Tell your family. Introduce them to the individuals at the nonprofit with which you have a relationship. I would be very careful not to convey the impression to your family that you expect them to give to your nonprofit champion. To the contrary, I'd acknowledge their own philanthropic interests, but I'd also ask that they respect your wishes. You can ask them to protect your requests after you are gone as a way to remember you.

CHAPTER 18

Assets to Fund Your Philanthropic Plan

Once you have identified the nonprofit object of your affection and assembled your team, the logical next step to developing your philanthropic plan is to consider what assets you will give to the nonprofit and how you will give them.

In terms of your team, your CPA and your financial planner will be best positioned to help you decide what assets to donate. Your CPA will understand which of your assets have taxable appreciation and by how much. Gifts to nonprofit organizations of capital assets will not trigger a tax on the appreciation of the assets, but instead you may qualify for a charitable deduction that is equal to the value of the capital assets at the time of the donation. For example, gifts of appreciated stock to a 501(c)(3) public charity will not trigger a tax on the appreciation but may instead create a charitable deduction for the donor based on the fair market value of the stock at the time of the gift. Understanding your capital assets, with a focus on imbedded tax liability, will give you insights into how to fund your philanthropic plan.

Likewise, your financial planner will help you consider your actuarial lifespan, your current and projected cost of living (including inflationary considerations), and your current asset base in relation to return. A good financial planner may not only help you better invest your wealth but may also help you understand which of your capital assets are more valuable to you in retirement or potentially less valuable in your estate. For example, if you die with an IRA in your estate, multiple layers of tax may be triggered. Alternatively, you might be able to roll over the IRA to a charity or name a charity as the beneficiary upon death and, in doing so, reduce tax liability from your estate.

Your financial planner can model for you the economic effects of a charitable gift annuity or a charitable remainder trust on your personal situation. With these types of vehicles, you may receive a payment stream for some period of years or the remainder of life, and thereafter the remainder interest passes to a nonprofit. If you make the arrangement irrevocable, you may be able to claim a charitable deduction at the time of funding. Depending on your life circumstances, these types of approaches to charitable giving can be quite effective.

This combination of disciplines, working with a financial planner and a CPA, can be an excellent way for a philanthropist to assess how best and with what assets to fund a philanthropic plan.

Categories of Assets

At first, identifying which assets will fund your plan might seem straightforward, but in reality, nonprofits are wary of any gift that is not cash. A mature nonprofit will conduct a fair amount of due diligence in connection with a noncash gift. A purpose of this chapter is to orient you to the concerns and typical responses of nonprofits when a donor proposes a noncash gift. For your consideration, the following are common examples:

SECURITIES

Securities are equity, stock, or ownership in a company. Securities can be either publicly traded or closely held.

Most nonprofits require that gifted publicly traded securities must be sold upon receipt unless otherwise restricted by applicable securities laws. If there are any restrictions on the sale of the security in the public market, a nonprofit might reject the gift. Generally, however, restrictions are few, and gifts of publicly traded stock are encouraged and accepted by nonprofits. They can easily be turned into cash.

Closely held securities are stock, equity, or ownership in a company that is *not* publicly traded. These include ownership in a mom-and-pop or local community business. Closely held securities often do not have a market for resale. When a 501(c)(3) organization becomes an owner in a closely held company that is taxed as a partnership or an S corporation, the nonprofit will likely incur unrelated business income tax from all net income arising from the closely held company. This may place the nonprofit's status as a 501(c)(3) organization in jeopardy. In many instances, nonprofits will decline a gift of closely held securities.

REAL ESTATE

Gifts of real estate may include a variety of property and ownership types, including developed property, undeveloped property, or gifts subject to a life interest. Prior to acceptance of real estate, a sophisticated nonprofit may require an environmental review of the property to ensure that the property has no environmental damage.

The due diligence of a gift in any interest in real property will often dig much deeper than environmental concerns. Nonprofits typically ask the following questions:

- Is the property useful for the mission of the nonprofit?

- Is the property marketable?

- Are there any restrictions, reservations, easements, or other limitations associated with the property?

- Are there carrying costs, which may include insurance, property taxes, mortgages, notes, etc., associated with the property?

Partial interests in real property, such as when a donor retains a life estate, often create a number of additional risks to the nonprofit. In cases of donor-retained life estates, expenses for maintenance, real estate taxes, and any property indebtedness must be paid by the donor and not the nonprofit. When those costs are not covered by the donor, the nonprofit is put in a difficult spot. If it pays for the donor's expenses, that action poses compliance risks to the 501(c)(3) status of the nonprofit. However, if these expenses are not paid, that creates risks to the property. Not a good choice either way.

TANGIBLE PERSONAL PROPERTY

This is a catchall category for miscellaneous in-kind gifts of physical assets. You probably now recognize the pattern of criteria the nonprofit will use to evaluate a gift of tangible personal property:

- Does the property fulfill the mission of the nonprofit?

- Is the property marketable?

- Are there any undue restrictions on the use, display, or sale of the property?

- Are there any carrying costs for the property?

It's easy to see that nonprofits love gifts of cash, while gifts of *things* can be challenging. A mature nonprofit will adopt a gift acceptance policy to address, in part, its risk tolerance to different types of in-kind gifts. Over time, experience should inform additions to the policy. You will find that nonprofits will use their gift acceptance policies as a softer means to decline a gift, often pointing to board policy to support their decision. As each of us develop our respective philanthropic plans, we should respect and consider our nonprofit beneficiaries' perspective on in-kind gifts.

As noted, the members of your philanthropic team with the skills to identify which of your assets to donate to charity are likely your CPA and your financial planner. Once you've figured out the funding sources for your philanthropic plan, it's time to consider the many ways you might structure your gift to a nonprofit. You are transitioning to development and documentation of your giving strategy. This transition often marks the moment when you will include your legal advisors in your planning, if you have not done so sooner.

CHAPTER 19

The Format and Drafting of Your Plan

Something wakes in a person when they seek the writing of the legal documents necessary to effect their philanthropic plan. I see this more and more with baby boomers and retirees these days. It's one thing to think of what you want to do. It's an entirely different thing to meet with professionals on your team to reduce your wishes to a binding document, agreement, or will. I want to acknowledge that feeling but to tell you to stay on mission. This is a necessary step to memorialize your philanthropic plan.

Your philanthropic plan may manifest in a variety of written documents. This variety relates to the types of assets being donated combined with your giving strategy, including whether you will include lifetime and/or planned gifts. I am providing below a list of giving strategies and related documents to consider in connection with any philanthropic plan. There are a few types of gifts that you can easily do on your own, but with others you may require professional assistance.

Gift Agreement

All gifts between donors and nonprofits are agreements, whether reduced to writing in the form of a contract or not. A nonprofit and donor may desire to enter into a formal, written gift agreement should they desire to document the terms and conditions of the gift. A gift agreement may specify details such as the purpose of all future distributions and, conversely, any restrictions on the use of the gift.

An important detail of all gift agreements is whether the document is binding or merely a nonbinding statement of intent. If it is binding, then the nonprofit may make a claim against you and your estate should you not fulfill the terms of the gift. If your binding pledge is large enough, the nonprofit will be incentivized to file a creditor's claim against your estate in probate court. I can attest to this, as I have filed many such claims.

Will

The will is the most commonly thought-of mechanism to effect a planned gift. A will is a legal document that specifies how your assets will be distributed after death. A bequest is a provision in your will that may designate a gift to a nonprofit. Often, wills identify a nonprofit as either a direct beneficiary with a specific bequest or a contingent beneficiary if all other beneficiary designations fail.

Every state has different rules about what makes a valid will, including how many witnesses and notaries must be in attendance at the signing. You should consult with an attorney to draft your will. Handwritten wills that fail the other requirements of state law will not be valid.

Trust Agreement

A trust agreement is a legal document that splits the ownership of an asset between two parties: the trustee and the beneficiary. The trustee holds legal title to the assets held in trust. The trustee may be paid for trustee-related services, but the trustee is not permitted to receive any benefit from the trust. The trust will name one or more beneficiaries who have the sole rights to receive the economic benefits of the assets held in the trust. Trusts can be either revocable by the creator or made irrevocable at or following creation.

Like a will, you can name a nonprofit as either a direct beneficiary of a trust or a contingent beneficiary if all other designations fail.

Charitable Remainder Trusts

Certain trusts are structured more specifically as philanthropic giving vehicles. Charitable remainder trusts, or CRTs for short, provide that the remainder beneficiary of the trust will be a nonprofit. There are two basic types: CRATs and CRUTs.

A charitable remainder *annuity* trust, or a CRAT, is an irrevocable trust. A CRAT lasts either until the donor dies or after a period of no more than twenty years. During the term of the CRAT, the trust will pay a fixed income to one or more designated noncharitable beneficiaries in the form of an annuity. The value of the annuity is calculated as a fixed percentage of the initial value of the trust's assets, and that amount must be no less than 5 percent but no more than 50 percent.[68] No further contributions are allowed after formation. When the term ends, any assets and funds remaining in the trust

---

68   See "Instructions for Form 5227 (2023)" at IRS.gov, accessed June 3, 2024, https://www.irs.gov/instructions/i5227#en_US_2021_publink10008805.

are transferred to the named charitable beneficiary(ies) and the trust concludes. Nonprofit beneficiaries may be either public charities or private foundations.

A charitable remainder *unitrust*, or a CRUT, is very similar to a CRAT. However, the key difference is that payments over the life of a CRUT may vary. Payments are recalculated each year as a fixed percentage of the current value of the trust assets.

Charitable remainder trusts work well when they are funded with highly appreciated property like public stocks, equity, and real estate. S corporation stock cannot be contributed to a CRT; however, partnership interests or C corporation stock may be placed in a CRT. There is no limitation on the amount of ownership that can be transferred. Here's an important rule of thumb: you will want to identify assets that create cash for distribution in order to support the payout requirement of the CRAT or CRUT. Assets that produce dividends and rents work well in a CRT. Illiquid assets may make it difficult to meet the distribution requirements and may need to be sold off and turned into cash at some point.

Charitable Lead Trust

Charitable lead trusts are the inverse of charitable remainder trusts.

A charitable lead trust is an irrevocable trust designed to provide financial support to one or more charities for a period of time. Charitable lead trusts operate for a term, which could be the life of one or more individuals. At the end of the term, the remaining assets of the trust are distributed to family members, other beneficiaries, or even back to the original donor.

A charitable lead trust can be created and funded either during the lifetime of the donor or pursuant to a will. A charitable lead trust can potentially provide benefits such as income tax deductions or estate or gift tax savings on assets ultimately passed to the individuals designated as remainder beneficiaries. At the same time, the trust distributes regular payments to benefit the named charity or charities during the term of the trust. This is an effective way to meet a significant annual giving commitment of a donor that might run over a course of several years.

However, there are a few drawbacks. Charitable lead trusts are not tax exempt. Taxes are levied upon the donor in connection with the trust's investment earnings. Because this type of trust is also irrevocable, following formation, the donor loses access to the funds and any income that the assets generate. Also, unlike a charitable remainder trust, it's usually not possible to change the charitable beneficiary of the trust. Charitable lead trusts are complicated. They carry ongoing "maintenance" costs, and they must be carefully planned to ensure there is enough money in the trust to make all the required payments during their existence.

Charitable Gift Annuity

A charitable gift annuity is a *lifelong contract*, not a trust, between a donor and a charity. At the time of the gift, the terms of the agreement will lock in the rate, amount, and timing of all payments that the donor (and spouse if they are giving as a couple) receive(s) for the remainder of life. Once the nonprofit receives the gift, it is set aside in a reserve account and invested. Based on your age at the time of the gift, you receive a fixed monthly or quarterly payout (typically supported by the investment account) for the rest of your life. At the end of the donor's life (as well as your spouse's if they're giving as a couple), the charity receives the remainder of the gift.

Life Insurance

It is possible for a donor to name a nonprofit as both beneficiary and irrevocable owner of a life insurance policy to effect a gift of a life insurance policy. With this type of gift, the donor pays all the premium payments on the policy. Such gifts are valued at their interpolated terminal reserve value, or cash surrender value, upon receipt. If the donor contributes future premium payments, the nonprofit will include the entire amount of the additional premium payment as a gift in the year that it is made. If the donor does not continue to cover premium payments on the life insurance policy, the nonprofit will be forced to either pay the premiums, convert the policy to paid-up insurance, or surrender the policy for its current cash value. In theory, this sounds like a pretty good gift, but in practice, I see most donors default on the payments, which places the nonprofit in the difficult situation of taking on a new, unbudgeted expense or losing the gift.

Life Insurance Policy Designation

Rather than try to give a life insurance policy to a nonprofit, it's easier to name a nonprofit as the beneficiary of your life insurance policy. This is a perfectly good planned gift. A life insurance beneficiary designation is simple to change and easy to effect. This is a move you can make on your own.

Retirement Accounts

Like a life insurance beneficiary designation, you may designate a nonprofit as a beneficiary of your retirement accounts, such as an individual retirement account (IRA) or a 401(k).

Additionally, individuals over seventy and a half are permitted to make a qualified charitable distribution of up to $100,000 each year from their IRA to a nonprofit. Such transfer does not trigger income tax to the donor but will generate a charitable deduction based on the size of the rollover. For those who are at least seventy-three years old, these charitable distributions count toward the required minimum distribution for the year.[69]

Bargain Sale

A bargain sale is the sale of a good or service to a charitable organization for less than the fair market value. In my practice, I see bargain sales occurring most frequently in the context of real estate. Often the sale price covers the donor's debt, but the equity is gifted to the nonprofit.

Most nonprofits will enter into a bargain sale arrangement only in instances in which the bargain sale furthers the mission and purposes of the nonprofit. Nonprofits will review many factors to determine the appropriateness of the transaction:

- What is the net value of the property being conveyed in relation to the gross value?

- Is there too much debt on the property, making the transaction no longer viable?

- Will the nonprofit use the property, or is there a market for sale of the property, allowing for a sale within twelve months of receipt?

---

69 "Qualified Charitable Distributions Allow Eligible IRA Owners up to $100,000 in Tax-Free Gifts to Charity," IRS.gov, November 16, 2023, https://www.irs.gov/newsroom/qualified-charitable-distributions-allow-eligible-ira-owners-up-to-100000-in-tax-free-gifts-to-charity.

- What are the estimated costs to safeguard, insure, and manage the property (including property tax, if applicable) during the holding period?

Other Legal Documents

Depending on the specific circumstances, other legal documents may be used to confirm various gifts. For example, if a nonprofit receives real estate or other property as a planned gift, the organization may require deeds, title documents, or appraisals to verify the gift. In connection with in-kind gifts worth over $5,000 made during a donor's life, for a charitable deduction to be permitted, the IRS requires the donor, the nonprofit, and a qualified valuation expert to sign a Form 8283, which attests to the value of the in-kind gift. Sophisticated nonprofits will require the donor to pay for and engage the qualified valuation expert and will ask the donor to indemnify the nonprofit in connection with the donor's tax reporting.

When you consider all these giving strategies and related documents, you can tell that the relationship of a philanthropist and a nonprofit working together collaboratively manifests in some form of a legal agreement. In many ways, you can describe the legal relationship as similar to a partnership. Partnerships are a two-way street. As a philanthropist, remember that not all gifts of noncash assets are in the best interest of a nonprofit. The same is likely true of giving strategies. If you are true supporters of the nonprofits that are your champions, you and your team should be oriented toward the maturity, experience, and perspective of the nonprofit you wish to support. When you are designing your philanthropic plan, you should check in with the nonprofit and the development officer(s) serving as your point of contact. Collaboration begins well in advance of the legal documentation of your gift. Your involvement of the nonprofit in your planning, by and through its development officers, will ensure that your plan may achieve the greatest impact possible in the long run.

CHAPTER 20

Endowment Giving within Your Philanthropic Plan

I n part 1, we proposed that a central role of the philanthropist in a democratic capitalist society is to restrict assets and wealth within the nonprofit sector. As we will examine, an effective means for a philanthropist to execute on that role is to make a gift to an endowment of a nonprofit organization that excels in organizational learning and retention of institutional knowledge. I believe in the due diligence associated with unrestricted giving—identifying the nonprofit organizations that excel in these two characteristics and trusting them with your gift. With endowment giving, we go one step further. We trust them with the corpus of our gift to maintain forever. We partner with them on a specific mission. After we're gone from this earth, the nonprofit carries our legacy forward. Trust is foundational in the relationship. This is why I like to highlight the examples of Alan and Joanne Moses, the Coastal Community Foundation, and the Beaufort Fund. This is trust-based philanthropy working at an ideal level.

Modification Provisions in Gift Agreements and Endowments

In my law practice, a common concern of the philanthropist when giving to an endowment is whether the nonprofit will unwind the endowment or raid the corpus after the philanthropist passes away. This issue can be addressed in the gift agreement with the nonprofit. You can restrict the nonprofit by contract from spending any principal of your gift indefinitely into the future. You may desire to do this to ensure that your foresight is followed even after you die.

If Fred Goff could advise you, though, he might tell you to be mindful that circumstances change over time. Any restriction that lasts forever, and that cannot be changed, may result in the gift agreement or endowment no longer functioning at some point. The purpose of the endowment may no longer have meaning or effect. I've seen funds that were restricted in the 1800s to fight yellow fever in the southeastern United States. There is no yellow fever anymore. I've seen these funds no longer able to make distributions. Here, you have charitable dollars locked up, unable to do any good or help anyone. That clearly can't be the result intended by the original donor. You don't want the icy grip of your cold dead hand to reach up from the grave to enforce a restriction that no longer has its original, or any, effect. A requirement of today may no longer be viable tomorrow. There is a delicate balance of protecting your plan to the maximum extent possible while recognizing an appropriate redirection when the charitable objectives are no longer viable. Interestingly, the default laws under UPMIFA provide guidance on this issue.

Under the "model" version of UPMIFA, there are four ways to amend an endowment:

1. The donor may consent.

2. Upon the request of a nonprofit, a state court may modify an endowment restriction regarding the management or investment of the fund if the restriction has become impracticable or wasteful, if it impairs the management or investment of the fund, or if, because of circumstances not anticipated by the donor, a modification of a restriction will further the purpose of the fund. The nonprofit must notify the state attorney general of the request, and the attorney general must be given an opportunity to be heard. To the extent practicable, any modifications must be made in accordance with the donor's probable intention.

3. Upon the request of a nonprofit, a state court may modify the purpose of the fund or the restriction on the use of the fund in a manner consistent with the charitable purposes expressed in the gift instrument if a particular charitable purpose or a restriction on the use of a fund becomes unlawful, impracticable, impossible to achieve, or wasteful. The nonprofit must notify the attorney general of the request, and the attorney general must be given an opportunity to be heard.

4. A nonprofit board may amend an endowment if it is more than twenty years old and less than $25,000 following notice to the state's attorney general of such proposed amendment.

After a donor dies, option (1) goes away. Options (2) through (4) become the only means to modify an endowment or institutional fund. However, in gift agreements today, many nonprofits are requesting the future right to modify the purpose or use of the gift *themselves* should circumstances change. Like many approaches to endowment giving, this type of *future-modification* provision was also pioneered by Fred Goff at the Cleveland Foundation. Nonprofits consider such a provision in a gift agreement as an advance "donor consent" under UPMIFA in compliance with option (1). An example of such a clause is as follows:

> If at any time following the death of philanthropist, the President of the Foundation certifies to the Board of Directors of the Foundation that the charitable purpose or any material aspect or provision of this Agreement has become unlawful, impracticable, or impossible to achieve, the gift may be used for such other purpose or purposes as may be designated by the Board of Directors, but only to the minimum extent necessary to address such issue, while seeking, in good faith, to preserve the intent and desires of the philanthropist to the maximum extent possible; upon receipt of such certification and alternate designation, the Board of Directors of the Foundation shall be authorized to amend or modify this Agreement.

Like anything, there are no black-and-white rules to philanthropy. The language above will give discretion to the nonprofit to decide if a change is warranted. Remember, forever is a mighty long time. The discretion of the nonprofit to make then-current operational decisions in connection with its endowments is likely necessary as you move forward decades and possibly centuries into the future.

UPMIFA provides a standard of fiduciary responsibility associated with the management of an endowment. In my mind, it is acceptable and often in your interest to simply rely on the law of the state. If you are not comfortable with the advance donor consent example above, tell the nonprofit that you wish the rules of UPMIFA to apply without any variation. UPMIFA provides external checks and balances in the form of attorney general and court oversight should a nonprofit desire to amend an endowment after your death.

Also, here is one detail about UPMIFA: it is state specific. You need to examine the version of UPMIFA that has been adopted in the state where the nonprofit is located. There can be variations that are different from what I'm describing in this handbook. Again, an attorney can advise you well on this issue.

What is also interesting about UPMIFA is that we're now seeing systems in state governments that are intended to enforce the rights of a philanthropist in a gift agreement, even after death. In our history of the United States, and humanity, this is new. It reflects a society that is placing importance on this issue, identifying a novel way to approach restricted charitable gifts, and memorializing our knowledge in the form of law.

CHAPTER 21

Your Message to the Future

I f you're lucky enough to wander the streets of Rome, perhaps heading from the Spanish Steps toward the Tiber River, and you find yourself walking the curvy, narrow alleys paved with blue stones worn smooth from centuries of footsteps before you, you may find yourself suddenly in front of the Pantheon, the Roman temple for all gods, originally commissioned by Marcus Agrippa during the reign of Augustus. The Pantheon was part of an aggressive building program of Marcus Agrippa. He started construction following the Battle of Actium in 31 BC, where Mark Antony and Cleopatra were defeated to ensure that Agrippa's father-in-law, Augustus, remained emperor of Rome. Although a fire in AD 80 significantly damaged the structure, Emperor Hadrian completed the temple forty-six years later in AD 126. It was Emperor Hadrian who transcribed on the portico of the Pantheon the following inscription:

M·AGRIPPA·L·F·COS·TERTIVM·FECIT

This translates to "Marcus Agrippa made this when consul for the third time."

And here we are, more than two thousand years later. We remain endowed with this temple to all gods, with the inscription still in place.

The memorial inscribed on the Pantheon is a moment carrying the memory of Marcus Agrippa forward across millennia. Just as Agrippa had the foresight to create such a building for Rome, Emperor Hadrian was able to send a message to the future, a reminder of Agrippa's life and his goal to create such monuments for the residents and visitors of Rome. Emperor Hadrian may have been linking himself to a period of time occurring a century and a half before his own life to show continuity to the time of Augustus, to an aspirational time.

This ability to name or memorialize some value or belief of the philanthropist is a meaningful tool, using foresight, to send a message across the ages. I've been lucky enough to stand in front of the Pantheon. I didn't know what the inscription meant when I first saw it. As a nonprofit lawyer, I've come to see the Pantheon as a public building with the inscription of a benefactor at the entrance. The fact that it has stood over two thousand years as a global monument for all humanity makes me feel more greatly the impact that can arise from giving to community. I get something of a similar feeling when a donor talks to me about their personal message. In the moment, you know you are experiencing something special with this individual.

The most personal part of the conversations with baby boomers or others who are thinking about their philanthropic plan, particularly as it involves their estate planning, is when they start talking about their perspective about giving. If there's one insight I've gained in life based on my role as a nonprofit attorney, it is this: everyone who makes a significant gift to a nonprofit has a personal message to express. I'm a bystander to those conversations, really. It's the development officer who has that conversation with you. I'm just taking notes and listening. But I hear it every time. I think this idea of a personal message is at the heart of the partnership between a philanthropist and their nonprofit champion. I understand there is a lot of technical theory involved to evaluate a nonprofit's organizational learning and institutional knowledge, and it's an entirely different discipline to plan a series of gifts involving wealth. But at the heart of the matter, we're talking about *you*. An individual. With a voice and a perspective—and a heart. Whether you keep it private or express yourself in twelve-foot lettering on the side of a building, you have a message in your philanthropy.

Naming Rights

Let's get back to basics and examine how naming rights are legally conveyed to a donor in connection with a philanthropic plan. Organizations will often want to honor or recognize a philanthropist with some grant of naming rights. Naming rights can be a valuable tool to you and a means to express your message.

An organization may bestow a grant of naming rights to a philanthropist to be transcribed upon any building, facility, monument, museum, performance hall, library, hospital, facility, or any component therein, or to any scholarship, fund, endowment, or fellowship. These inscriptions are sometimes referred to as "philanthropist graffiti." This is a moment of acceptable indulgence where you call upon the future to remember some individual or idea. You may identify yourself or a loved one. With enough room (and a large enough gift), you may inscribe a Rosetta stone of information.

Nonprofits today understand that a naming opportunity on a physical asset should be time limited. Buildings in the United States are not quite like the Pantheon. Nonprofits are more aware that there will come a time when no building will exist to carry the inscription or name. Nonprofits often see naming opportunities as a replenishing inventory of charitable assets, attractive from one generation of philanthropists to the next. A sophisticated nonprofit will time-limit naming opportunities associated with a building or physical assets in its gift agreements and reserve the right of the board, in its discretion, to tear down the building and remove the naming right should a change in circumstance warrant.

I'm not going to lie and say that a philanthropist's desire to place their name on a building doesn't have some element of self-indulgence and ego. There will always be a transactional component to giving, with perhaps the rare exceptions like Alan and Joanne Moses, who named their fund after their community while remaining anonymous during life.

I offer that your message to the future isn't really what you name a building anyway. Yes, you can write some wisdom for the future on the side of a building, and some do, but your message to the future is more than that. It's in your actions. Your identification of a cause and a nonprofit champion is an expression of your identity. It is that with which your empathic heart and head identify. Your gift reflects your foresight. When you give like this, you set an example, even when you're anonymous. All these actions reflect your message to the future, whether or not you are conscious of it.

Remembering Those We Love

Many times, it's not your name that you'd like inscribed on the walls of a building endowed for the use of generations to come. The death of a loved one is the greatest pain and suffering in the human experience. Whether a death is unexpected or follows a lengthy illness, the absence of a loved one is a void in your life. Philanthropy can be a means to fill that void. Your message to the future can be an expression of love for someone who has made an impact on your life or whom you dearly miss. This is another way philanthropy can heal you.

You may use your philanthropy to dedicate a memorial to a loved one, whether living or deceased. How much more meaningful is it to see a plaque at a performance hall, library, university, or hospital than to visit a gravestone in a cemetery? Memory is so important to us. Preserving the memories of the ones we love as soft reminders for the ones that follow is a desire of human nature. It reflects our love for one another. There's a healing power in the philanthropic way.

Your message to the future can be so many different things. It doesn't have to be a physical monument. It can be the creation of a scholarship to a university, an endowed chair in a symphony, or a fund dedicated to eradicating a disease. Consider your feelings about the sudden loss of a parent or child. Now imagine establishing an endowed scholarship at that person's alma mater that looks for recipients who may embody some spirit of your loved one and some interest in a common field. Maybe you ask to meet these recipients. Maybe you have a chance to interview potential candidates and make recommendations. Maybe you can see a glimmer of your loved one in a student. This experience allows you to honor the memory of one who is no longer with you but whom you miss. It allows you to *pay it forward* with their memory and enable their memory itself to continue to have an impact for generations to come. In these times of loss and suffering associated with the finality of death in this material world, the philanthropic experience has the power to heal.

In your gifts and your endowments for the future, you can leave any message that you wish from your experience. As a philanthro-pist, I know that you will speak from a place of empathy, truth, and foresight. At the end of your life, this can be the message that you leave behind. What words will you choose?

CHAPTER 22

Why We Are Philanthropists

I t is estimated that around 107 billion humans have lived on planet Earth since the emergence of homo sapiens three hundred thousand years ago. This number is based on many factors, including estimates of population growth rates over time and the lifespan of early humans. These estimates are subject to a great deal of uncertainty depending on the assumptions used in the calculations. Still, 107 billion is a number that we can comprehend. Actually, it seems low to me, given the level of current human achievement. Step inside a children's hospital in any significant urban center, and you will witness wonders of human technology that cure and heal such diseases and injuries that would have been fatal more than one hundred years ago … a blink of the eye in the three-hundred-thousand-year history of our species. If you also consider that, as of this writing, there are just over 8 billion humans in the world, that means 7.5 percent of all humans ever in existence are currently alive.

Everywhere around us, we inherit the legacy of all those humans. We stand today upon the accomplishments or failures of those who came before us. We didn't just hit a triple when we were born on third base. Understanding our place in the history of our species can enable each of us to see beyond our deaths.

For some of us, we will immediately know our mission. The direction of our philanthropic plan manifests itself as we overcome traumas to address injustices in our society. These might be personal traumas or traumas for which we've been called to bear witness.

For others, we need to continue our journey in the philanthropic way for our mission to manifest.

If we were in ancient Greece and heard someone say, "Because of philanthropy, Prometheus gave man fire," we might hear a deeper meaning. Isn't it just as true to say, "Because of a profound love of humanity, Foresight endowed humanity with language, from which knowledge emerged to create civilization and technology"? This is the archetype on which the philanthropist is based.

Philanthropists understand their collective place in the continuum of human history. Philanthropists employ empathy and foresight, with an ethic of information and truth, to restrict asset bases in a democratic, capitalist society, with a goal of ensuring the advancement of technology benefits humankind fairly and safely. Technology so often emerges from the blind pursuit of wealth. But as philanthropists, we can balance those advancements and shed light on darkness through an ever-greening investment in community.

A philanthropist pursues mission in terms of multiple generations and perhaps the span of humanity. A philanthropist's success ensures that our communities can be built on a rising awareness of moral obligations to one another. Unjust disparities can be reduced and possibly eliminated. A safety net can be woven into society in a manner that is external to government and that can thrive from one generation to the next, notwithstanding any politics of the day. Philanthropists are the gardeners of democratic capitalistic societies, ensuring that a robust portion of the economy is dedicated to public vision, through purposeful restriction of assets pursuant to our respective philanthropic plans. Philanthropists plant trees in the form of nonprofits and endowments in our capitalist landscape to bless the future of humankind long after they are gone. People often complain that it is rare to find happiness in life, but it doesn't have to be. Happiness exists in the philanthropic way.

The Philanthropic Way

As we pursue the philanthropic way, we seek to cultivate the virtue of philanthropy within ourselves through empathy, the ethics of information and truth, and foresight. We cultivate these disciplines through visualization exercises, such as projecting love to individuals for whom we are grateful, remembering and writing down the times when someone was generous to us and when we were generous to someone, and thinking about the vast technology that is embodied in basic construction elements of our homes, machines, and the world around us. We express thanks and gratitude for the world, the people in our lives, the people who came before us, and the many endowments we have inherited. We have a responsibility to seek the truth through lifelong learning, with the hope that the pursuit of knowledge will drive foresight.

This should be the mindset when you engage with nonprofit organizations. With all nonprofits, as philanthropists we assist them in the ongoing practice of organizational learning coupled with the memorialization of institutional knowledge. This is an evangelism of philanthropy as we build capacity in the sector while restricting significant asset bases for public and community benefit.

All these philanthropic activities will provide meaning to your life. What is inescapable to all of us, however, is that life will come to an end. Death meets each of us in our own time. It is through a contemplation of death that you as a philanthropist may consider the scope of your philanthropic plan and the meaning that you have imposed upon your time here. The pinnacle of all philanthropic plans is the planned gift. As this handbook advocates, the most impactful of planned gifts may be to an endowment of a mature nonprofit organization with a sophisticated level of organizational learning and institutional knowledge. Endowment returns over long periods of time should reflect increasing intergenerational equity, pursuant to an investment strategy that might include mission- and program-related investments. The income of such an endowment should generate consistent distributions annually to support the organization, with income added each year to the corpus to stay ahead of inflationary pressures.

I think the future of philanthropy in the United States will be trust based. I see a world where philanthropists will increasingly focus on the establishment of endowments designed to support the general operations of nonprofits. Once fully funded, those nonprofits will become perpetual actors in our society, working to harmonize advancements in technology with community values. The accumulation of greater amounts of restricted wealth in more and more nonprofits may be the natural trajectory of democratic capitalist societies. While it may take a long time, the projected trendline makes me think that the nonprofit sector will continue to expand its economic influence on American society for the foreseeable future. And it may be inevitable that nonprofits will dominate the markets. Nonprofits of perpetual existence may even amass a majority of the wealth in the United States. How will we respond to an increased nonprofit presence in the marketplace with investment strategies that include mission-related investments? What will society look like when the distributable income from these endowments becomes significant in relation to GDP? Will lawmakers look to tax these funds for the first time, or will the influence of the nonprofit sector change our politics for the better? Time will tell.

As philanthropists, we should remind ourselves of our role in the great continuum of human history. Be mindful of these moments when you claim this view of humanity, even for a second. Those moments provide valuable perspective to life. As philanthropists, we look to the Promethean archetype as an example of human-love, self-sacrifice, and a desire to endow humanity with ever-increasing advancements in knowledge and technology. Be thankful for the world endowed to you. In times of prosperity, plant trees of economic hope in our capitalist landscape. Work so those who follow may see a forest of such trees.

I wish you well on your journey in the philanthropic way. May you find the happiness of a generous heart.

AFTERWORD

I n the spring of 2019, a series of events led me to envision *The Philanthropist Handbook*. My wife and I met a couple at a dinner party in March of that year. They had recently retired and moved from Boston to our hometown, Charleston. As we got to know them over dinner, they told us they'd taken a class on how to retire prior to their move to Charleston. Among the tips they learned, they were advised to consider seeking community engagement through local nonprofits. Volunteer activities can be an opportunity to meet new people and to fill the newly "released" hours of the day. At first, my wife and I thought it was funny to take a class in retirement, but the idea lingered with me. I realized that if I were to retire tomorrow, I would fail abysmally at it.

A few weeks later, in April of that year, my wife and I traveled to Palm Beach, where I had been nominated by a good friend to join the International Beefeaters Society, which is a dinner club with ties to the Palace Guard in London. The group meets for dinner twice a year to enjoy good food and company. Over the weekend, I was given a handbook of the rules to be a Yeoman Warder of the Club. The handbook was very tongue-in-cheek and reminded me of the Time Life "how to" books on things like plumbing, carpentry, and electrical wiring that I'd inherited from my grandfather.

On the plane back to Charleston, my mind merged the conversation with the couple who took a class in retirement and the Beefeater club handbook, and the result was the initial idea for *The Philanthropist Handbook*. I began to think of being a philanthropist as a job, or a role, or an identity … something like going from Joe Blow to becoming a Yeoman Warder. I wondered if you could teach anyone to be a philanthropist, whether they were looking to succeed in retirement or otherwise.

Why philanthropy?

Philanthropy, or rather assisting philanthropists, is my job. I am a tax attorney, and over the years, my legal practice began to focus almost exclusively on nonprofit organizations. But while it started as a job, over time it turned into something else. It's hard not to be changed as you listen to individuals who carry a passion and love for others, who genuinely care about people, like the kinds of folks you encounter in the nonprofit sector.

Working with nonprofits, I saw certain individuals—often behind the scenes, sometimes anonymous like Alan and Joanne Moses—who were able to effect great things through profound empathy and foresight. As a lawyer, I've seen money affect people—for both good and bad. Money is like Miracle-Gro. Sprinkle enough of it on someone, and it will augment their personality, either in unfortunate, self-indulgent ways that never lead to fulfillment or happiness, or sometimes, with some people—those who think of others before themselves, or perhaps as equal to themselves—money will enable them to reach different heights in life, largely by giving them a means to really help others.

Andrew Carnegie articulated a vision of philanthropy in his essay "The Gospel of Wealth." A wealthy individual should "consider all surplus revenues which come to him simply as trust funds, which he is called upon to administer, and strictly bound as a matter of duty to administer in the manner which, in his judgment, is best calculated to produce the most beneficial results for the community …"[70] We are lucky to live in a world where there are so many individuals who share this way of thinking.

In 2010, Warren Buffett and Bill and Melinda Gates launched the Giving Pledge. The pledge is a commitment for some of the world's wealthiest individuals to contribute the majority of their wealth to philanthropic causes during their lifetime or as a planned gift upon their death. Since its launch, more than two hundred individuals and families from around the world have signed this pledge, including Mark Zuckerberg, Richard Branson, Elon Musk, Larry Ellison, and MacKenzie Scott. Signatories of the pledge commit to using their wealth to tackle some of the world's most pressing issues, such as poverty, inequality, disease, and climate change.

Here's the funny thing about most of these people: they derived their wealth from information technology. These are the titans of the age of information.

I appreciate these people. They have created this century's technology and aided the progress of humankind. What I wonder is this: As they grow older, will they have the transformations of heart, like Carnegie and Rockefeller, their counterparts from the age of industrialism, to turn their profit toward healing the unfortunate side effects of their wealth accumulation?

I also wonder whether these billionaires will transfer significant portions of their wealth to public charities, as MacKenzie Scott is doing through trust-based philanthropy. Or will they transfer their

---

70   Andrew Carnegie, "The Gospel of Wealth," *The Nature of the Nonprofit Sector, editor J. Steven Ott (Boulder, CO: Westview Press, 2001), p. 68.*

wealth to private foundations that employ their children as officers? There's a difference there, you know.

Either way, if you think about it, if they make good on the Giving Pledge, that's an additional supercharge to accompany the wealth transfer of the baby boomer generation. My imagination gets me thinking of a world where a majority of the wealth of the United States is controlled through endowments held by nonprofit organizations. If the trendline of nonprofit wealth accumulation continues on its current course, that is a possibility.

On a different level, I don't think the signatories on the Giving Pledge mean to be elitist. I appreciate the values behind the pledge, but I also recognize the inherent injustice in so few having so much philanthropic power. Nevertheless, this movement harkens to values held in societies that flourished in the ancient world. And it doesn't limit us from asking or pursuing this question: How can each of us share in that philanthropic experience? And if more of us, perhaps all of us, could walk from time to time in the philanthropic way, the positive impact to humanity would be exponentially greater.

So my thought on that plane ride from Palm Beach to Charleston in the spring of 2019 was this: *How might I help others learn about philanthropy and, if possible, discover a philanthropist identity within themselves?* I wanted the idea to be aspirational for everyone, and I didn't want anyone to feel excluded, given some of the baggage the term *philanthropist* might carry. In my mind, I wanted to make it fun, like my handbook becoming a Yeoman Warder. I was also thinking about those retirees who may want to take a class on philanthropy to give them a new vision for retirement or students who desire to direct their social media pages toward campaigns to support charitable causes instead of birthday gifts. I was thinking about lonely individuals who might discover themselves in volunteering, and I was thinking about all those individuals who have been helped by others and want to give back. I was thinking about the baby boomers who are the drivers of the greatest generational transfer of wealth never before seen in the United States.

My initial writing was focused on how to help someone assess a nonprofit organization when contemplating a donation or considering a volunteer opportunity. Then 2020 occurred, and many things changed. The last time there was a global pandemic was in 1918, with the Spanish Flu. My grandfather, John Clay Grayson, from whom I inherited those Time Life how-to books, was born on December 14, 1919, in Muhlenberg County, Kentucky, that same blue-green region, stripped by coal mines, that John Prine sang about in many of his songs. If my grandfather were alive today, he would have no memory of that pandemic. However, that would also make him 104 as of this writing, when in fact he died in 2002 at the age of 82. So even if he could recall stories from his parents, perhaps of fears during his mom's pregnancy in rural Kentucky, my grandfather had passed away almost two decades before the emergence of COVID-19. I have friends who had children during 2020 and 2021. I imagine feelings of parents were no different no matter the century. Such is human experience. But it's curious what we remember and pass on to our children and which experiences, for whatever reason, we forget.

For a more introverted person like me, the COVID-19 years gave me greater time with my thoughts. I became inspired, more out of boredom and looking for something to do than anything else, and I began to write the handbook in earnest. Likely a result of my legal training, I found myself approaching the topic of philanthropy by trying to define the word itself. I had no idea that seeking the etymology of *philanthropy* would lead me to consider Prometheus as an archetype of the human psyche, that philanthropy is a component of our nature, and that our survival as a species has depended on it.

With the COVID-19 pandemic in the rearview mirror, an initial draft of the handbook was nearing completion. The book wasn't what I'd expected five years before. The hubris is not lost on me, writing a book entitled *The Philanthropist Handbook* when my own empathy and foresight fall so short. But that's not the point of this book. If there were a point, it's to give you a moment when you might reflect on the big picture, to view your life in its entirety, and to see yourself in the continuum of human existence. We all face death, each doing so with various beliefs about what comes next, with faith but no empirical data. And yet, as we view the conclusion of our respective lives, most of us are faced with profound questions: What was my mission in life? How might I be judged? I'm not the most empathetic, and I can't see into the future, but that doesn't mean that I can't try. I can identify with the characteristics and aspirational goals of a philanthropist, take up that mantle from time to time, and, in the days to come over the course of my life, make more moments count—really count. That's what I hope for you too.

www.ingramcontent.com/pod-product-compliance
Lightning Source LLC
Chambersburg PA
CBHW031428270326
41930CB00007B/619